STOP the CHAOS

How to Get Control of Your Life by Beating Alcohol and Drugs

Allen A. Tighe, M.S., C.C.D.C.R.

Illustrations by L. K. Hanson

HAZELDEN®

Hazelden
Center City, Minnesota 55012-0176
1-800-328-0094 Outside the U.S. and Canada, and the Virgin Islands)
1-651-213-4590 (FAX)
http://www.hazelden.org

Library of Congress Cataloging-in-Publication Data

Tighe, Allen A., 1944–
    Stop the chaos: how to get control of your life by beating
alcohol and drugs/Allen A. Tighe; illustrations by L. K. Hanson.
        p.   cm.
    ISBN 1–56838–282–0
    1. Alcoholism—United States—Prevention. 2. Drug abuse—
United States—Prevention. 3. Alcoholis—Rehabilitation—United
States. 4. Narcotic addicts—Rehabilitation—United States.   I. Title.
HV5292.T55 1998   98–46624
362.29'18—dc21   CIP

04 03 02   10 9 8 7

Cover design by Spaulding & Kinne
Interior design and typesetting by Spaulding & Kinne
Illustrations by L. K. Hanson

About the author

Allen A. Tighe, M.S., C.C.D.C.R., has worked in the health care field
for thirty-five years. With fourteen years' experience in continuing care
and relapse prevention, Tighe currently serves as clinical supervisor of
Hazelden's continuing care program. He's the creator and presenter
of Hazelden's quarterly four-day relapse prevention workshops and
a counselor for relapse prevention continuing care groups.

CONTENTS

INTRODUCTION

This book is for anyone who needs information and guidance about alcohol and drug addiction, including people who are concerned about a loved one's drinking or drugging. It's for people who aren't quite sure whether they have a problem with their chemical use and for people who've tried to stop using.

Many people view alcoholism and drug addiction as a weakness or a moral issue. Research has shown the true nature of addiction. It affects all types of people—men and women, young and old, rich and poor. Alcoholics and addicts *lose the ability to control their chemical use because of brain chemistry changes.*

Addiction is also a family disease. Alcohol and drug users create chaos not only in their own lives but also in the lives of family and friends. Addicts or alcoholics may be so wrapped up in denial that they refuse to look at the destruction. Family and friends are confused, hurt, and desperate for an answer. Reading this book can help loved ones to understand addiction and ultimately to learn how to help themselves.

The disease of alcohol and drug addiction can be treated. Alcohol and drug addiction, or chemical dependency, is a progressive and potentially fatal disease. Addiction is a complex process. Treating addiction likewise requires a multifaceted approach that addresses the mental, physical, emotional, and spiritual aspects of a person.

This book identifies symptoms of alcohol and drug abuse and dependency and the changes needed for a return to a healthy, meaningful life without chemicals.

For the chemical user, these questions are answered:

- Do I really have a problem with drugs and alcohol?
- What is addiction and how does it work?
- What can I do to stop or to moderate my own chemical use?
- What do I do when I can't stop using alcohol or other drugs?
- What changes do I need to make in my life to stay sober and how do I make them?

For family and friends, these questions are answered:

- Why does my spouse/partner put drinking and drugging ahead of the family's needs?
- If he or she loved me, wouldn't they quit?
- What can I do to get my husband, wife, partner, or friend to stop using?
- Why do I feel crazy living with someone who's abusing alcohol or other drugs?
- How can we rebuild our relationship?

Regardless of the drug of choice—whether it be heroin, Valium, vodka, or beer—every addict and alcoholic has a chance at a new life. And everyone, including family and friends, benefits from the peace and serenity that recovery from addiction provides. ***Stop the chaos now.***

Chapter 1

Am I an Addict or Alcoholic?

 ongratulations on deciding to explore chemical abuse and addiction. If you're reading this book, you probably have many questions concerning alcohol and other drug use.

Many people first become concerned about their alcohol or other drug use or that of another person because of some negative consequence. Legal difficulties resulting from driving while intoxicated, assault, or domestic violence may bring attention to a chemical problem. Loss of employment or broken relationships may also lead us or others to question our use of chemicals. Frequently a family member, friend, or employer may say something about the amount of our drinking or drugging. These are signs for us to take a closer look at our chemical use.

I was going to have only a couple, but I ended up having about eight.

Example 1. College fraternity members may drink heavily on a regular basis. A keg in the frat house may be customary. These members frequently become intoxicated and rowdy. They may be labeled as "real drunks." They may even have some consequences from their chemical use. Yet, when they graduate from college, they get married, have children, and stop or moderate their use of drugs or alcohol.

Alcohol and other drug use is part of our culture. Many people in the United States use alcohol or other drugs socially. Many others don't use alcohol or other drugs at all. They just don't seem interested. In the United States

1. about one-third of the population abstains from (does not use) alcohol and other drugs;
2. about one-third uses occasionally on a social basis;
3. about 25 percent abuses alcohol and other drugs;
4. the remaining 6 to 8 percent of the population has crossed the line into addiction.

If we are *social users,* we can take it or leave it. If we are *chemical abusers,* we may go through a stage of consuming intoxicating amounts and then moderate, or limit, our use or lose interest. If we are *addicts,* we lose control of our chemical use and continue to drink and drug despite negative consequences.

It's difficult to accurately assess the level of abuse or addiction in ourselves or someone we know. Anger, fear, denial, and concerns about what others may think can make us misinterpret or "play down" what we see. Many of us may also be concerned about being labeled an "addict" or "alcoholic."

The line between chemical abuse and chemical dependency confuses most people. We need more information on the differences between social use, chemical abuse, and chemical dependency.

Can *I* Take It or Leave It?

Some of us question whether we really have a problem with alcohol and other drugs or are just "social users." Social users rarely have consequences associated with alcohol or other drug use. They have little desire to use alcohol or other drugs to intoxication. They may say, "Oh, I hate that feeling of being out of control." They may leave a drink half finished. Their lives do not revolve around chemical use. The people they associate with are unlikely to be heavy abusers or addicts. Alcohol and other drugs simply are not an issue in their lives.

Not All "Drunks" Are Alcoholics

Not all people with alcohol or other drug problems are alcoholics or addicts. Some people may consume large amounts of drugs or alcohol, appear intoxicated on many occasions, but may not be dependent on those chemicals. They lack the spiritual, emotional, psychological, or physical dependence associated with addiction.

[see example 1]

Everyone has heard of people who drank, drugged, or smoked cigarettes excessively and then one day, out of the clear blue, decided to stop. They seemed to have no problem quitting. For them, quitting was a matter of willpower and determination. These people hadn't crossed the line into addiction.

Chemical abusers are just that—people who use chemicals in an abusive manner. If abusers start to experience negative consequences because of their chemical use, they can decide to moderate or stop. Programs are available to help them make those decisions.

There are ways to help us determine whether we're abusing chemicals. One important way is to listen to what others say to us about our alcohol and other drug use. Often, those close to us see our situation more clearly than we do.

[see examples 2 and 3] ☞

Check the appropriate box in response to the question. If you answer yes to any of the questions, consider taking a close look at your chemical use.

PERSONAL STORIES

Example 2. Ben spent his weekends smoking marijuana. He seemed to see few of his old friends. On several occasions, his wife had made plans for the family, but Ben never felt like participating. He missed out on his children's school and athletic activities. Ben's wife told him he seemed to prefer "a joint" to his family. Ben shrugged his shoulders and thought, "No wonder I smoke with all the complaining around here."

Example 3. Brenda's mother commented that Brenda seemed to be drinking a lot more now than she had previously. Brenda said there was a lot more stress in her life now and she needed to relax. She believed her mother wasn't being sympathetic to her problems.

	YES	NO
1. Has a friend or family member expressed concern about your use?		
2. Has your social life changed or have you switched friends?		
3. Have you experienced a negative consequence from your use? Legal? Emotional? Physical?		
4. Do you find that your behavior changes when you use chemicals?		
5. Are you using chemicals to become more outgoing or to overcome fears?		
6. Do you go against your values or morals when you use alcohol or other drugs?		

Be honest. Rationalizing behavior or consequences or making excuses will only hinder you from receiving help. Show these questions to someone who knows you well. Be willing to listen to what others may tell you about your use. Others may see changes that you don't. Remember that abusive drinking and drugging take a toll on the body and emotions. This is reason enough to take a hard look at your chemical use.

✧✧✧

We need to take some time to consider the serious and life-changing consequences of continuing to abuse chemicals. Abuse, left unchecked, could progress into addiction. We can decide to moderate or stop our chemical use. It becomes *our* choice. We can get help by contacting a chemical abuse program that specializes in helping people moderate their alcohol and drug use.

Crossing the Line into Addiction

Addiction is a complex disease with psychological, environmental, social, spiritual, and physiological components. How do we know if we have crossed the line into addiction? Do we identify with having problems with alcohol or other drugs? Remember this important point: We don't willingly choose to be addicted. Most people don't want that label or the lifestyle. Because of the stigma, we're not anxious to admit to having *any kind* of problem with drugs or alcohol.

Addiction knows no age or gender restrictions. Rich or poor, old or young, regardless of intelligence level, everyone is susceptible. Many alcoholics and addicts started out as social users. They progressed to abusive users. Their level of abuse increased. Somewhere along the way they "crossed the line" into addiction. Some became addicted early into their use, perhaps almost immediately. Others used for years before experiencing problems. They wonder how they could have used for so long without consequences and then suddenly spiraled downward.

Where are we along that sequence? Have we tried to convince ourselves that we are social users? Do we really have a problem with alcohol or other drugs?

There is no laboratory test for addiction. We look instead at our behavior and thinking. If we are concerned about addiction, we need to be rigorously honest.

Answer the following questions as honestly as possible.

	YES	NO
1. Have other people talked to you about your alcohol and other drug use?		
2. Have you experienced legal, work, family, or relationship problems because of your use?		
3. Have you quit using for a month or a week to prove you could and then started again?		
4. Does it seem that you need more or use more chemicals now than you used to?		
5. Have you ever experienced a loss of memory while using? For example, maybe you can't remember driving home after drinking or what you said or did at a party.		
6. Do you spend a lot of time thinking about using drugs or alcohol during the day?		
7. Have you tried to stop using but couldn't?		
8. Have you lied to others about your drinking or drugging or tried to hide your use?		
9. Have you ever regretted what you've done while using?		
10. Have you started to withdraw from others to protect your chemical use?		
11. Do you use drugs or alcohol to cope with life?		
12. Has your chemical use ever put yourself or others in danger?		

Answering yes to three or more of the questions in exercise 1b *may* indicate that you are addicted to chemicals. You need to get a professional assessment of your chemical use. *An accurate assessment is essential.*

In talking to a professional, we need to be *rigorously honest* about our alcohol and other drug use. If we try to minimize our use or deny our consequences, we only hurt ourselves. Professionals have talked to many people like us; they are there to help, not to criticize or judge. They themselves may be in recovery from drugs and alcohol and truly understand what we are going through.

Common Traits of Addiction

Addiction has three main characteristics: loss of control, denial, and preoccupation.

Loss of Control

Those of us addicted to mood-altering chemicals don't have the luxury of making a choice about our chemical use. The biggest difference between abuse and dependency is that, as alcoholics and addicts, *we have lost the ability to control our chemical use.* We say that we are *powerless* over alcohol and other drugs. Powerlessness means being unable to predict or to control when we use or how much we may use at any given time.

Three DUIs isn't THAT bad. I'll just have to be MORE CAREFUL, that's all.

- We cannot foresee the outcome when we start to use drugs or alcohol.
- We cannot predict how much we will use. A pledge to just "stop for a minute at the local bar" or to just "have a couple" turns into an entire night of drinking or drugging.
- We find ourselves needing to use more and more—a condition called *tolerance.*
- We have vowed to quit our use on several occasions but have been able to stop only for a short period or not at all. We tell ourselves that if we can stop for three months, we are not an addict or alcoholic. If we accomplish our goal, we immediately go back to drinking or drugging.
- We find that when we drink or drug, our behavior becomes unpredictable. We may violate our social or moral values. We do things that we would not consider doing while sober.

Denial

A major obstacle to recognizing our addiction is denial. We tend to minimize or deny the effect our dependency has on others or ourselves. We minimize or lie about the amount of our chemical use. This behavior allows us to protect and continue our alcohol and other drug use while preventing us from looking at the seriousness of our problem. We make excuses, explain away consequences, or blame others for our chemical use. We end up being the last to know how severe our alcohol and other drug use has become. Denial can be

1. refusing to accept that we're alcoholics and addicts. We still see chemical use as an option.
2. minimizing the severity of our dependency and what we need to do to stop our use. We try to control our use.
3. ignoring the problems we've created because of our use.
4. focusing on other people's faults rather than on our own.
5. refusing to acknowledge people, situations, and events that cause us stress. We may deny the need to take action to resolve problems.
6. believing that we can live with some dishonesty in our lives. Secrets or lying by keeping silent become habits for addicts and alcoholics.

[see examples 4 and 5] ☞

Raoul and Susan each have a belief system that minimizes or denies the real scope of their alcohol and other drug use. Addiction is progressive. If these individuals do not get help, they will begin to suffer severe consequences. Yet, their denial holds them captive. They may have to suffer major consequences before acknowledging they have a problem. Denial prevents us from taking an honest look at our problems with drugs and alcohol.

Example 4. *"I've been stopped for DUI on three occasions, but I had a good lawyer each time." Raoul may have had a good lawyer, but he does not face the fact that he is drinking to intoxication and driving. He thinks if he "beats the rap," he can continue his dangerous behavior. He denies that his drinking is a problem because he has avoided legal consequences.*

Example 5. *"Sure, I have a drink once in a while, but I never have more than a couple drinks and never during the week." In reality, Susan is frightened and being dishonest. She drinks almost every day and her amount is rising rapidly. She tries to act normal when her children come home from school. She worries that if her husband or family finds out, she might end up divorced and separated from her children. She's thinking that because she cannot seem to quit, there is something morally wrong with her. Her refusal to acknowledge the problem is based on fear.*

Example 6. At work, Woody found himself concentrating on going to the bar for happy hour that day. His boss had commented on his lack of focus on his work. Woody was counting the hours. He thought about how long it would be before he could drink again. As the afternoon went on, his anxiety grew. He projected how exciting this evening would be. He could hardly wait to leave the office and rush to his car.

Example 7. Betsy knew that her roommate was leaving for the weekend. It was the perfect opportunity to use chemicals without interruption. She had spent a week planning for this time. She had made sure to have enough cocaine. She had hidden her drugs with care so her roommate wouldn't find them. She had lied to several friends about her plans for the weekend so she could be alone. Betsy tingled with anticipation as she said good-bye to her roommate.

Preoccupation

Another factor in addiction is the preoccupation that alcoholics and addicts have with their chemicals. Preoccupation means that we spend a great deal of time anticipating, planning, and protecting our chemical use. Thoughts of using fill our minds constantly.

Anticipation of pleasure is combined with the fear that somehow our plans will go astray. How, when, and where can I use next? How can I avoid trouble? Do I have enough of my drug of choice or should I be getting more? This type of thinking illustrates what our priorities really are. Our performance on the job or our interactions with friends may suffer, but we don't want anything to interfere with our use of alcohol or other drugs. Chemicals take priority over our families and our health. Our drug and alcohol use come first.

☞ *[see examples 6 and 7]*

Preoccupation includes obsessing and planning our chemical use while attempting to protect our next "high." *We want to make sure that we're able to do what we want to do when we want to do it.*

Not Every Alcoholic Is a Falling-Down Drunk

Some of us conclude that we can't be an alcoholic or addict because we don't believe we have had any consequences of our chemical use. We don't seem to fit our own image of what an alcoholic or addict is.

- We may hold responsible jobs. We may even be quite successful.
- We always show up for work.
- We are well liked by other employees.
- We have no legal problems. ("I can't be an alcoholic! I've never had a DUI.")
- We say, "I never drink before noon."

The above statements are typical of functional alcoholics or addicts. If we are functional alcoholics or addicts, we are able to get along in society while continuing addictive use of chemicals. We have not yet experienced the heavy consequences of our use. We are on borrowed time. The progression of our illness will ultimately bring us down.

Some of us drink or drug periodically. We abstain for various amounts of time and then go out on a "binge." When we start our use, we experience loss of control. We drink or drug for the purpose of intoxication. We cannot predict the outcome of our use, and we may suffer consequences frequently. We may say, "I can't be an alcoholic; I don't drink every day." Nevertheless, we are truly addicted.

Not all of us look like the stereotypical addict or alcoholic. Whether we're chronic users with severe lifestyle consequences, binge users who plan our using experiences, or functional alcoholics or addicts whose friends and co-workers may be unaware of our using, the same principles apply. We all have the terminal, progressive illness of addiction. Our consequences will become increasingly more severe and our emotional, spiritual, and physical health will deteriorate. We will not be able to regain the ability to drink or drug normally again.

We cannot overcome our addiction by ourselves. Willpower and strength of character will not play a role. We have lost control of our chemical use. We have become powerless over our addiction.

Remember:

- There are different levels of chemical use: social using, abusing, and dependency.
- We need to be honest about our alcohol and other drug use. Being an alcoholic or addict has nothing to do with our worth as people. It's not a matter of weakness or moral failure. It's a matter of having a progressive illness that leads to serious legal, social, and physical consequences.
- We need to listen to what others are telling us. Because of our own minimizing and denial, we have difficulty seeing how serious our condition may be.
- The three main traits of addiction are loss of control, denial, and preoccupation.
- If there is any indication of a chemical-use problem, we need to seek professional help. Alcoholics and addicts can live spiritually sound and successful lives, but we must take certain precautions. Treatment, counseling, or self-help groups can provide a basis for recovery.

Notes

Chapter 2
What Is Chemical Addiction?

Accepting that we're dependent on drugs or alcohol is hard. We find we don't fit our idea of an addict or alcoholic. Old family values, cultural beliefs, movies, and television shows have given us inaccurate pictures of alcoholics or addicts. These images have influenced our thinking. We may see people who are chemically dependent as losers or failures, or as people in the gutter of life, which is certainly not the way we want people to see us.

Dispelling Old Myths

The terms *addiction, addict,* and *alcoholic* carry a stigma, or feeling of shame. Many people believe that

1. addiction is a weakness (if we were just morally or emotionally stronger, we could "lick" this problem);
2. we should be able to stop using on our own;
3. we just don't have enough willpower (if we were more disciplined, we'd be able to drink or drug in moderation).

Don't buy into these myths. People who've never encountered the true nature of addiction can't conceive of what we're going through. They've never experienced the inability to stop chemical use. They just don't understand. The response of our loved ones and close friends can be particularly hurtful.

We may see our addiction as unfair. No one ever said to us, "Hey you! Stand in this line if you'd like to become addicted to alcohol or drugs and ruin your life." We weren't given that choice. We ask, "How did I end up this way? Why am I the one who has to be like this?" We see dependency as a curse in which we had no say. Somehow, we became dependent—but how? To answer these questions, we need to understand the addiction process. Its origin is deeper than poor control of our impulses.

How Did *I* Get Addicted?

Addiction to drugs or alcohol is a complex illness. It is progressive and can be life threatening. In addition, it has social, physiological, and psychological components. Several factors increase the risk for addiction.

- *Drug availability.* The more available drugs and alcohol are, the more likely we are to take them. Even if mood-altering chemicals aren't readily available, we'll find them if we really want them.
- *Purity and route of administration.* The purity of the drug and the route of administration (how we take it) determine the level of euphoria and how quickly we can reach it. Chemicals that give us a quick and powerful high are more likely to be rapidly addicting. Purity of the drug includes the amount of alcohol (proof) in a beverage.

Inhaling and injecting quickly transmit the chemical to the brain, producing almost instant euphoria. Swallowing drugs and drinking are slower to produce the high. The quicker the euphoria, the more likely we are to repeat our drinking and drugging.

- *Dose, frequency, and duration of use.* This factor has to do with the amount of drugs we take, how often we do them, and over what length of time. Some drugs are more quickly addicting than others. While we may avoid the quick dependency to crack cocaine, using alcohol and other drugs over a sustained period can lead to addiction.
- *Genetic factors.* Certain groups of people and certain families seem to have higher levels of addiction than others. In some families almost all members may be chemically dependent. Genetic makeup seems to influence susceptibility to addiction.
- *Developmental factors.* As we grow up, we develop our own attitudes about drug and alcohol use by observing chemical use in our families, in society, and in our peer groups.
- *Mental health disorders or chronic pain.* Those of us afflicted with certain mental health conditions have a higher rate of addiction than the general population. People who have chronic pain may abuse pain medications in an effort to feel better and may eventually become addicted to these medications.
- *Psychosocial factors.* When people have meaningful alternatives to chemical use, the incidence of abuse and addiction is lower. Having sober places to socialize and a variety of drug-free entertainment options seem particularly important for teens and preteens.

The Brain Chemistry of Addiction

When we put mood-altering drugs (which includes alcohol) into our bodies, our bloodstream quickly carries these intoxicating chemicals to our brains. In the brain, drugs set off complex chemical reactions and activities that can distort our sense of reality. We know this altered state as being intoxicated, or getting "high." Some of us find this feeling pleasurable and worth repeating. Other people find getting high an unpleasant experience and, as a result, will seldom use alcohol and other drugs.

Contemplating the Brain

You have No IDEA of the mysteries I hold.

Uh, OK...

Addiction is not about willpower or weakness. Research has shown that the addiction process is connected to how our brains are "wired." Powerful chemicals called *neurotransmitters* control brain activities. These neurotransmitters carry messages from one brain neuron to another. The levels of these neurotransmitters can vary depending on how much and how often we use alcohol and other drugs.

Figure 1: The Brain

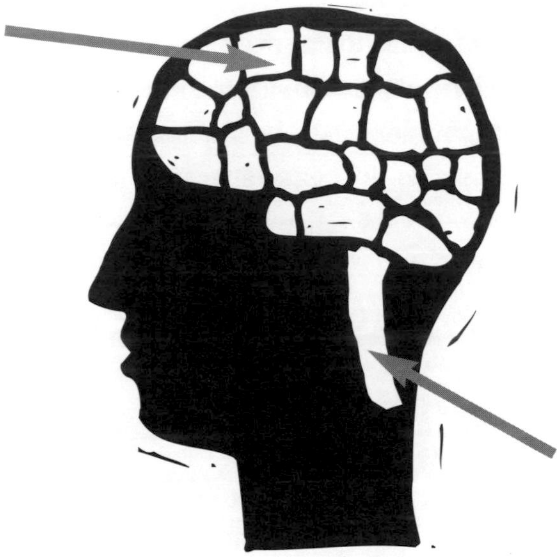

The cerebrum is the thinking area of the brain: "I know I will never take another drink or drug. I know I'm strong enough to be around drugs or alcohol."

The brain stem, or primitive brain, is home to the limbic system and is the automatic area of the brain. The limbic system contains the components of our addictive nature.

The process of addiction takes place in the limbic system, which is located in the brain stem (see figure 1). The limbic system stimulates our sense of smell, motivation, sex drive, and complex emotional responses. It also plays a role in regulating basic bodily functions and other actions that are automatic—actions that occur without thought. The automatic nature of the limbic system sets up the addiction process. Let's look at the following: the pleasure center, automatic recall of emotions and memories, and thinking versus the limbic system.

The Pleasure Center

To understand addiction, we need to understand the pleasure center. Located in the limbic system, the pleasure center responds to pleasurable stimulation and learns to repeat it. Neurotransmitters, including endorphins and dopamine, activate the pleasure center. Alcohol and other drugs increase the activity of neurotransmitters, resulting in the high—our feelings of euphoria. As shown in figure 2, we set up a cycle.

Figure 2: The Pleasure Center Cycle

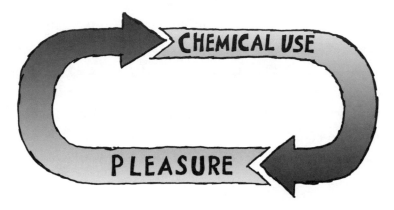

We learn to repeat this pattern. If some is good, more must be better. As we continue using our chemicals, our *desire* to repeat this pattern develops into a *need* to repeat the pattern. Our bodies become accustomed to having drugs and alcohol present. Our brains stop producing neurotransmitters on their own; they come to rely on alcohol and other drugs to produce the "feel-good" chemicals.

Without our drugs, we feel lower than low. Our brains are waiting for the drugs and alcohol to do the work, and we're waiting for our brains to do their job. Our bodies are out of balance. We experience cravings for our chemicals as we go through psychological and physical withdrawal. Our need to use alcohol and other drugs becomes more powerful than our thinking processes that say we shouldn't.

PERSONAL **S**TORIES

Example 8. Elaine had been in a
chemical dependency treatment
center for addiction to cocaine.
She had never experienced consequences from alcohol use so,
after she got out of treatment,
she began to drink periodically.
Within a short amount of time,
she noticed that her drinking
had escalated. She soon found
that she could not control her
alcohol use. Elaine recognized
that she had now become
dependent on alcohol.

Crossing the Line into Addiction

We may have heard others say that they drank or drugged for years
without harmful consequences of their use. Then one day they somehow
"crossed over the line"—they became unable to control their chemical
use. Crossing the line is when our brains adapt to our chemical use and
override our rational, or reasonable, thought processes. The chemical
use–reward sequence that leads to the euphoria in the pleasure center
becomes "hardwired," or imprinted, into our brains. Once this occurs,
normal drinking and social drug use are impossible. We've crossed the
line into addiction. We're no longer able to control our use.

Cross-Addiction

People who are chemically dependent do not crave particular drugs,
but rather they crave the euphoria that a drug produces. While each
of us may have our favorite drug, we're actually addicted to the feeling
of intoxication. *This means that we can become easily addicted to any
mood-altering drug.* If we find ourselves addicted to one chemical, we
will not be able to replace it with controlled use of another chemical.
When we decide to stop using, we must decide to stop using *all* mood-
altering chemicals.

☞ *[see example 8]*

Elaine found that she was susceptible to other mood-altering
drugs. It would not be unusual to learn that alcohol use led Elaine
back to her drug of choice—cocaine. Chemicals lower our inhibitions.
One of our inhibitions is to avoid our drug of choice.

Progression

Addition is a progressive, terminal disease. Left unchecked our
addiction can take our lives—either through accident or from physical
complications. As we start to look at our drug and alcohol use, we
believe it's unlikely that we could ever get that bad.

What we may overlook is the progressive nature of our illness.
Our alcohol and drug use becomes progressively worse over time. As
we build up a tolerance to alcohol and drugs, we have to use more
chemicals to get our high.

The higher the level of toxic mood-altering chemicals in our body,
the more damage that is done to our organs and nervous system. Our
liver, for example, has a harder time detoxifying our chemicals. We no
longer function in a normal manner. Our health starts to deteriorate.

Though we try to control our use, our consumption rises. Even if we stop using for a period, we quickly end up back where we left off. Some of us who return to using find we're worse off than when we stopped. It's as if the disease kept progressing even though we had stopped our using. Progression makes our addiction that much more dangerous.

Automatic Recall of Emotions and Memories

The automatic recall of emotions and memories makes staying sober more difficult. We have heard of Vietnam veterans who have post-traumatic stress disorder (PTSD). A classic example would be a veteran who's walking down the street and hears a car backfire. He immediately perceives the noise as an incoming artillery round and throws himself on the ground, overwhelmed by the "flashback" of past feelings and emotions that seemingly came out of nowhere.

This situation illustrates the automatic activation of past emotions and memories from some unexpected trigger. We may have experienced this ourselves. Hearing a song we listened to on our first date can immediately bring back nostalgic memories and perhaps a tear. Or the smell of fresh baked goods may trigger memories of Grandma's house and the warmth and safety there.

Automatic triggers can bring back memories and feelings of our using experiences. Our bodies may also react to these triggers. Many alcoholics and drug addicts salivate while watching a chilled beer in a TV commercial or experience an intense craving while watching drug scenes in a movie.

EXERCISE 2a

What situations or people trigger using urges for you? Try to identify as many situations or people as possible. Write them on the lines in the box that starts below and continues on the next page.

_____

_____

_____

_____

_____

_____

_____

_____

Thinking versus the Limbic System

Is just knowing that we're an addict or alcoholic enough to keep us from using? Experience shows that knowledge that we're addicted will not stop us from drinking or drugging. The thinking portion of our brains may tell us that we shouldn't drink, but the automatic recall of memories and emotions combined with the hardwiring of the brain will override those thoughts.

Many addicts and alcoholics who quit using are surprised by the profound intensity of the urge to return to chemical use. The idea that they were dependent and could not use chemicals seemed to vanish when confronted with the using urge. The knowledge alone that we're alcoholic or addicted to drugs will not prevent us from using again.

Remember:

- Addiction is not a matter of strength or moral character. It's not about being weak or bad. Addiction is a complex illness.
- Our brains adapt to our chemical use by allowing drugs and alcohol to influence the production of neurotransmitters, the natural "feel-good" chemicals of the brain. Once our brains stop producing these chemicals on their own, we've crossed the line into addiction.
- The hardwiring of our brains and the automatic recall of emotions and memories ensure that we cannot rely on rational thinking to keep us from drinking or drugging.

Chapter 3
AM I READY FOR RECOVERY?

ow do we know if we're ready to "recover"? We may have agonized over whether to stop using alcohol and other drugs, but stopping our chemical use is not the hardest part. Like the smoker who says, "Quitting is no big deal; I've quit hundreds of times," the person addicted to alcohol or other drugs has the most difficulty *staying off* mood-altering chemicals. Maintaining our abstinence requires serious personal changes.

What Does Recovery Mean?

For our purposes, to *recover* means to restore ourselves to a healthy emotional, physical, and spiritual condition—free of alcohol and other mood-altering drugs. We seek to reclaim the life we've lost through our addiction. Recovery is the *process* of returning to a healthy and fulfilling lifestyle. Recovery is not a destination but a lifelong journey. Recovery from addiction encompasses

1. stopping our chemical use completely
2. admitting we're powerless over our addiction
3. understanding we have a chronic illness
4. making the necessary changes in our lifestyle
5. asking others for help
6. being patient

Stopping Chemical Use

After we've decided to recover, the first step is to stop using all mood-altering chemicals, including alcohol. When we stop using, we begin detoxifying our bodies. As the body gets rid of toxins, or poisonous chemicals, and begins to rebalance itself, we experience uncomfortable withdrawal symptoms.

Our experiences during withdrawal depend on the drug we're withdrawing from and on how much we're used to taking. Withdrawal from certain chemicals can be mild and hardly noticeable. Withdrawal can also create severe, life-threatening reactions.

We need time to adjust to the absence of chemicals. This detoxification period can be only a few days, as with alcohol, or much longer, as with drugs such as benzodiazepines (Valium, Xanax, Klonopin).

If we're taking a prescribed medication, we can check with our doctor to determine whether it's mood altering. *It's important not to stop the use of prescribed medications without the approval of a physician.*

We should never try to detoxify alone. Alcoholics and addicts can die during withdrawal. The wisest course of action is to seek professional care from a treatment facility or a physician who is familiar with detoxification from mood-altering chemicals.

We may need medications to prevent seizures or to slowly detoxify our bodies. A medically supervised withdrawal is the best way to ensure safety and to avoid suffering from unnecessary symptoms. Once we are stable, we can embark on our journey.

Now that I know all these things, and I don't use anymore, I MUST BE CURED!

Admitting We're Powerless over Our Addiction

It's difficult to accept that we've encountered something we can't control. This admission is crucial. Until we can accept on a daily basis that we can't control our drug and alcohol use, we're doomed to repeat failed attempts at controlled use. When we don't accept our condition, we deny or minimize the amount of effort needed to maintain our recovery.

We invite trouble by using intellectual processes to analyze and to understand our addiction. We assume that our newly found knowledge will overcome our old thinking and behavior. When we stop chemical use, our lives and our thinking are still programmed to enable alcohol and other drug use. These old patterns are not erased easily and can return automatically.

Understanding We Have a Chronic Illness

Addiction is forever. It's neither a moral weakness nor a matter of willpower. Addiction is about brain neurochemistry and adaptations our bodies make to our chemical use. The illness of addiction is chronic—it's ongoing and with us for life. Just hoping it will go away doesn't work.

Our addiction has a biological basis. Some refer to addiction as a disease or illness. Just as diabetics have to monitor their chronic condition on a daily basis to avoid a reoccurrence of diabetic symptoms, the alcoholic and addict need to monitor their chronic condition on a daily basis. If we ignore our addiction, we will once again experience the symptoms of chemical use—irrational thinking and behavior. A return to chemical use can follow quickly.

Making the Necessary Changes

We'd prefer to stop our chemical use without having to make many lifestyle changes. We picture ourselves going back to a "normal" lifestyle. We forget that the lifestyle we were leading was anything but normal. Lifestyle changes may be the most difficult part of recovery.

[see example 9] ☞

Example 9. *Alicia had made a commitment to her counselor to stop her alcohol use. She quickly found, however, that many of her social activities revolved around drinking. Alicia decided to continue socializing with her old friends and just not use alcohol or other drugs. After all, she had made the promise to her counselor and knew that her chemical use had brought her nothing but problems. Soon after, while attending a party, Alicia began to listen to friends who tried to persuade her that she was not really an alcoholic. She decided that she would have only a few drinks. That night Alicia ended up arrested for driving while intoxicated.*

Alicia believed that she could safely continue her contact with people who abused drugs and alcohol. She believed that she could choose whether to drink. All of us in recovery need to change the direction of our lives. Our old lifestyle won't keep us sober. We need to find new outlets for our time and activities that don't include mood-altering chemicals. Necessary changes may involve

1. staying out of bars, clubs, and liquor stores
2. staying away from old using friends and others who abuse alcohol and other drugs
3. not contacting our drug source for *any* reason (Throw those telephone numbers away!)
4. keeping away from areas where we know drugs are available
5. not keeping alcohol or other mood-altering drugs around the home or office

Asking Others for Help

When we were using drugs and alcohol, we frequently thought we knew all the answers. We believed we were in control of our lives.

In early recovery, we realize that our chemical use dictated our lifestyle. We used chemicals to get through life. We discover we're lacking basic coping skills and the knowledge needed to get through this period. We have difficulty dealing with normal life issues, much less with the wreckage of our addiction.

Our insides shout that somehow we must accomplish our recovery by ourselves. We see asking for help or discussing feelings as an admission of weakness.

We soon discover, however, that we can't stay sober alone. We need to acknowledge the importance of getting strength and guidance from others in recovery—we need to acknowledge that they know more about recovery than we do. Recovering people become the most powerful tool we have in recovery. We can use this tool in important ways.

- We can share our thoughts and feelings with other recovering people. Still having using urges is normal and does not reflect on our seriousness to stay straight. We can talk about our urges with people who've been there.

- We can admit that others know more than we do about recovery. We don't know all the answers.

- We can listen to others' stories about their recovery and learn from their experiences.

Being Patient

We often have great expectations of others and ourselves in early recovery. We're convinced that our lives will quickly change for the better. We want to get on with our lives and prove ourselves to others. We view the time spent in our addiction as wasted and wish to put the past behind us. We need to make up for lost time.

People in recovery need to remember that everything happens in its own time. Recovery is a process. As addicts and alcoholics, we have a tendency to try to force the square peg into the round hole. When it doesn't fit, rather than search for a more rational solution, we simply get a bigger hammer.

By trying to move too fast, we create frustration and resentment because things don't go *our* way or happen at *our* pace. These feelings and our lack of perceived progress can lead us back to chemical use. Developing an attitude of patience and acceptance enables us to deal with these stressors.

How Do I Know If I'm Ready to Recover?

Some of us are pressured into abstinence when legal or family consequences become too severe. We may not see the role that drugs and alcohol have played in our lives and have no real intention of quitting. We comply to avoid further conflict or consequences.

Some of us see that our lives are becoming increasingly chaotic and unmanageable. We're aware that something is wrong. We're willing to stop chemical use to see if our lives improve.

It's of little consequence how we get to the point of considering stopping our chemical use. The important part is that we're *willing to take a look at our use.* Most of us are not completely convinced that recovery is the answer. We hear ourselves making statements such as the following:

- I'm not sure I'm really that bad. I'm not like those other people.
- Do I want to do this? What if I try to quit and fail?
- Drugs and alcohol are my best friend. How will I cope without them?
- I don't need to abstain. I can just drink and drug less often.
- Isn't there an easier way to do this?
- I don't want to be an alcoholic or addict.

Few of us are willing to accept overnight that we are addicted to alcohol or other drugs. Most of us are willing to admit that we might have some type of problem with drugs or alcohol. The evidence is usually there. What we don't understand is the severity of our problem. Even if we firmly believe that others are wrong about our chemical use, we need to listen to what they're saying and to continue to gain knowledge about alcohol and other drug addiction.

There is no magic. A willingness to listen and to explore our chemical use is the essential part of starting recovery. We must keep an open mind. If we find we are addicted to drugs and alcohol, we're ready to do whatever it takes to stay sober.

EXERCISE 3a

On a separate sheet of paper, write a personal history of the consequences of your chemical use.

---

1. Identify times when you missed appointments with friends, family, or clients.

2. How does your behavior change when you use chemicals?

3. Identify times when you've tried to control your use and ended up using more than you planned. Be honest.

4. How many times were your problems caused by chemicals?

5. When have people commented on your use?

Get friends and family to help. Exploring your chemical use will help you see it more clearly.

Exercise 3b

Ask yourself the following questions.

	YES	NO
1. Am I willing to examine my use of mood-altering chemicals?		
2. Am I ready to make genuine changes in my lifestyle?		
3. Do I believe that I need the help of others to stop my chemical use?		

If you're not sure how to answer the above questions, keep reading and try to keep an open mind. Deciding to start recovery could be the biggest decision of your life.

❖❖❖

Remember:

- Recovery is a process. We need to be patient.
- Many of us may have trouble believing we're addicted to chemicals. It's important to keep an open mind. We may not see how severely our addiction has affected us.
- People in early recovery need to be careful of withdrawal symptoms during the detoxification period. We need to get professional help or guidance.
- We need to be willing to listen to what others say to us about our behavior.
- We need to ask others for help and guidance.
- Our addiction is a chronic illness that may worsen if left unchecked.

"It was the best of times, it was the worst of times."

Charles Dickens,
A Tale of Two Cities

Notes

Chapter 4

UNDERSTANDING THE RECOVERY PROCESS

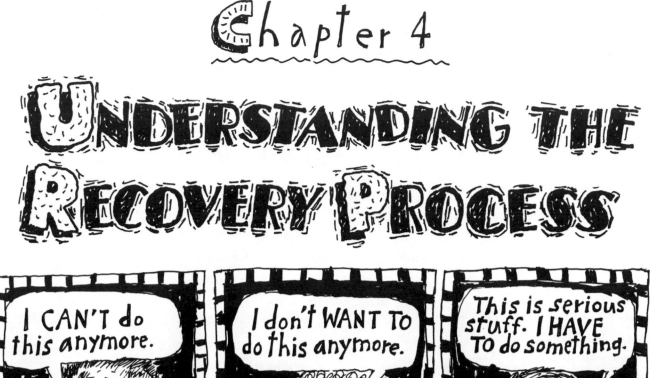

ecovery is a dynamic process. It's composed of stages that most of us will encounter on our journey. Each stage has its own development and solutions. For some of us, certain stages may present problems that are particularly hard to resolve. Or, we may find that the stages are relatively straightforward. These stages build on one another. Some require us to learn coping skills. Others reveal distractions in our journey of recovery. Our individual path is determined by the severity of our addiction and by social, environmental, and psychological factors.

Before we can build a foundation for recovery, we need to do three things:

1. Stop using mood-altering drugs and alcohol
2. Begin to develop a "recovery" attitude
3. Accept the severity of our addiction

Abstinence and Attitude

Next to abstinence, one of the first steps in the recovery process is developing a new outlook. An attitude that fosters drug and alcohol use will not help in our quest for recovery. Stopping our chemical use is not enough. We must change ourselves.

When using, we didn't fully acknowledge the effect our chemical use had on ourselves and others. We were interested only in maintaining our using lifestyle. We were self-centered and blamed others for our problems. Dishonesty was deeply ingrained into our nature. We often failed to take responsibility for our actions.

In recovery, we replace our self-seeking lifestyle with one of acceptance of others and ourselves. We focus on gratitude, personal responsibility, and honesty. Our goal is to be mature and honest with ourselves and to integrate emotional and spiritual growth and healthy interactions with others.

Recovery means dealing with the reality of how drugs and alcohol have affected our lives. It means changing our attitude, our approach, and our lifestyle: friends, social activities, living situations, or employment.

☞▌ *[see example 10]*

Abstinence without a program of personal growth is not likely to result in long-term recovery. Quitting drugs and alcohol may actually be easier than changing our attitude and behavior. Accepting responsibility for our behavior and making the necessary changes is difficult. We need to follow a simple plan combined with patience.

[see figure 3] ☞

The scope of the changes we need to make depends on how much damage our addiction to drugs and alcohol has caused. We need to learn some principles for developing a healthy recovery attitude.

Example 10. *Karen had used drugs and alcohol for years on an increasing basis. Over that period, she had developed an adversarial attitude toward her co-workers and boss. Her chemical use had negatively influenced her ability to do her job and to get along with others. She appeared angry and judgmental. People kept their distance from her. Karen decided to stop her chemical use. She did nothing, however, to change her attitudes. Her co-workers noticed that while she had improved her attendance and was more productive, she was even more angry and hostile than before. Many of them wished she had continued her chemical use since her hostility while using was more predictable. A co-worker told her, "You were easier to get along with when you were drinking." Karen was shocked at this statement.*

Figure 3: Starting the Recovery Process

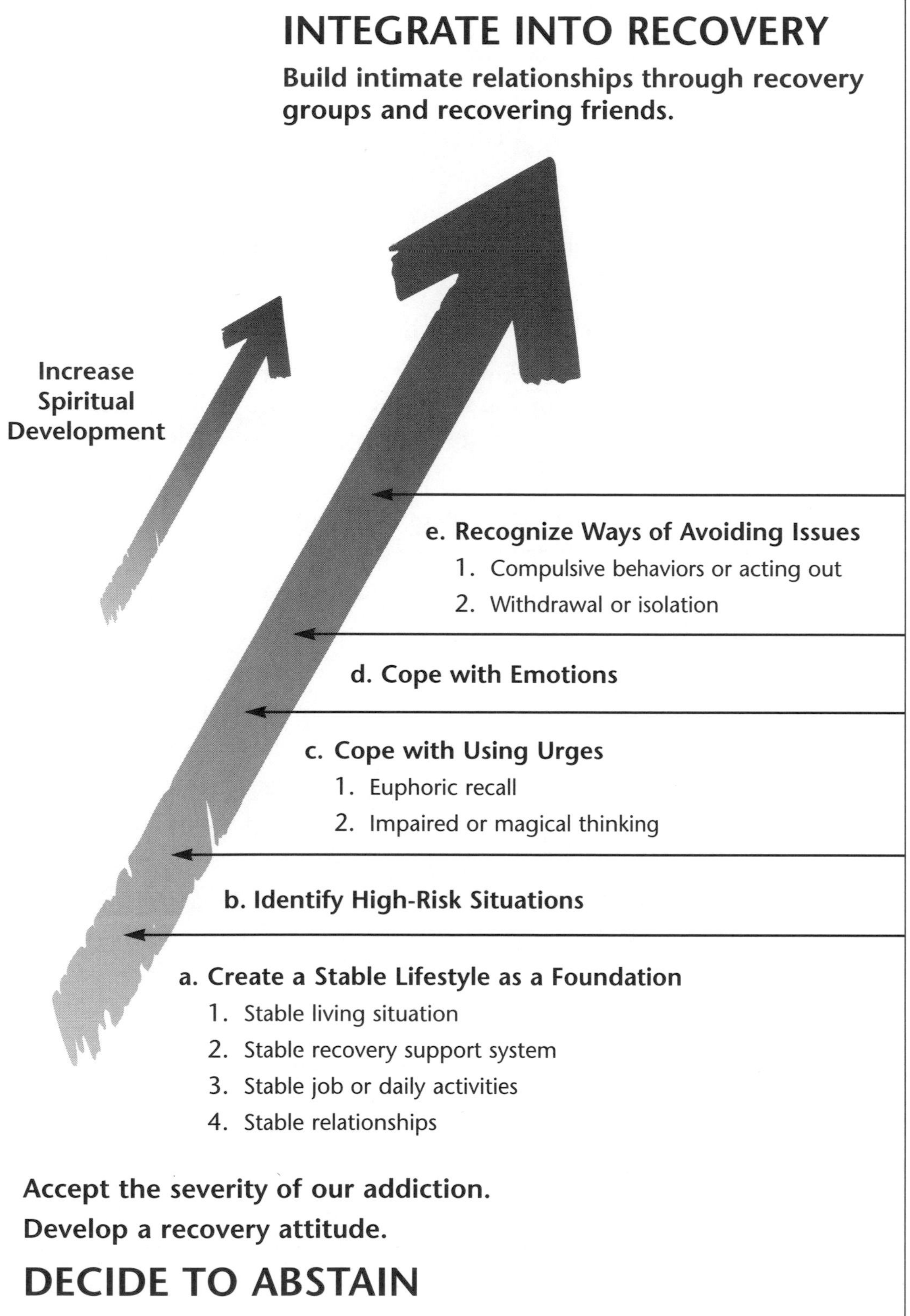

INTEGRATE INTO RECOVERY
Build intimate relationships through recovery groups and recovering friends.

Increase Spiritual Development

e. Recognize Ways of Avoiding Issues
1. Compulsive behaviors or acting out
2. Withdrawal or isolation

d. Cope with Emotions

c. Cope with Using Urges
1. Euphoric recall
2. Impaired or magical thinking

b. Identify High-Risk Situations

a. Create a Stable Lifestyle as a Foundation
1. Stable living situation
2. Stable recovery support system
3. Stable job or daily activities
4. Stable relationships

Accept the severity of our addiction.
Develop a recovery attitude.

DECIDE TO ABSTAIN

HOW

The letters *HOW* stand for Honest, Open, Willing. This acronym reminds us of what it takes to accept responsibility for our actions so that we can stabilize our lives.

- *Honesty* is a prime factor in our journey. We need to be honest with others but, more importantly, *with ourselves.* Our chemical use resulted in a lifestyle based on denial and dishonesty. We need to face the extent of our addiction and its effect on others. We must approach our journey with intense purpose and honesty.

- *Openness* is one of the more challenging parts of recovery. We may fear that if others really get to know us, they will reject us. "What will someone think if I tell them about who I really am and about what I'm really feeling?" We may see openness as giving others an advantage over us. One way to get around these fears is to start by being open with people who are in recovery. They understand. They've been there before and have the wisdom to guide us through our troubles. We can also be open to what they say.

- *Willingness* is our commitment to recovery. We need to be willing to do whatever it takes to protect our sobriety. We're still somewhat unaware of the flaws in our behavior and thinking. We listen to others for insight about ourselves and our addiction and do not dismiss their advice. We accept that others have a better perspective on us than we have on ourselves. We're willing to take action on that advice. Our first reaction is "No one understands me. *I know what I need to do.*" If this were true, we would have resolved our dependency long ago.

In recovery, as in life, we frequently encounter problems. Some of these are unexpected and leave us overwhelmed and anxious. When this happens, we can remember that persistence pays off. A statement from Calvin Coolidge, thirtieth president of the United States, can put our journey into perspective.

"Nothing in the world can take the place of persistence. Talent will not; nothing is more common than unsuccessful men with talent. Genius will not; unrewarded genius is almost a proverb. Education will not; the world is full of educated derelicts. Persistence and determination alone are omnipotent. The slogan 'Press On' has solved and always will solve the problems of the human race."

— Calvin Coolidge, 1932

Persistence is an important message in recovery. Returning to chemical use or to old behaviors and thinking is not uncommon. Let's not be discouraged. We can't let momentary setbacks defeat us. A common theme in recovery is "two steps forward, one step back." We need to return to our basic support system for answers in times of stress. Family members, friends, and others in recovery may see our progress long before we ourselves are able to see and feel the effects of the changes we're making in our lives.

Accepting the Severity of Our Addiction

Many of us new to recovery can now see the obvious—that our drug and alcohol use caused negative consequences in our lives. But most of us have not yet realized the extent and power of our addiction. We continue to think that we'll have some degree of control over our chemicals, that our knowledge of our dependency will enable us to make rational decisions concerning our use. We forget the role of the limbic system and of automatic emotional and memory recall in our addiction (see chapter 2).

We say to ourselves that we have wasted a lot of time with our chemical use. We feel the need to prove to our families and ourselves that we're not the "black sheep" we perceive ourselves to be.

[see example 11]

Tom's exhibiting a common thought pattern. He believes that now that he's sober he can quickly regain lost time. It hasn't occurred to Tom that he has never developed study skills. He has never faced life without drugs and alcohol as a buffer. He doesn't yet possess the skills for independent living. Although Tom's not prepared for the challenge of college, he believes that by enrolling, he's doing something positive for himself.

In early recovery, we may want to put the past behind us or to forget about our mistakes. We find ourselves wanting to move forward quickly. This type of thinking minimizes the true impact our addiction has had on our lives. Addiction is not something we can now discard because we understand that we can no longer use drugs and alcohol.

PERSONAL STORIES

Example 11. Tom is thirty-one years old. He has spent the past fifteen years doing drugs with his friends. Most of his high school classmates have gone to college and have good jobs. His brother and sister are both attorneys. Tom completed less than a year of college before he dropped out. He has two months clean now. He is considering returning to college next month. He believes he has to catch up with his classmates and prove to his family that he is a competent individual.

As part of our new lifestyle, we begin to realize just how much we depended on chemicals. We can find ourselves quickly slipping back into old attitudes and behaviors. We start to recognize that knowledge of our addiction or fear of consequences will not keep us sober. *We must allow ourselves time to develop new skills and attitudes. We need to be patient.*

Creating a Stable Lifestyle as a Foundation

Once we've dealt with abstinence, attitude, and acceptance, we can begin building a stable foundation. Without one, our recovery is at risk. We can divide the building of our foundation into four separate areas:

1. Developing a stable living situation
2. Building a stable recovery support program
3. Stabilizing our job or daily activities
4. Developing stable relationships

Stabilizing these areas gives us the best chance for sobriety while we gather the essential experience, knowledge, and skills to maintain our recovery. We attempt to "clean house" of things that pull us back to chemical use. The less stable our foundation, the more likely we are to return to chemical use.

☞▊ *[see example 12]*

Lori saw that she needed to make major lifestyle changes if she were to stay off drugs. This thought was frightening. The changes seemed overwhelming. She wondered if there were an easier or softer way to attain sobriety. We, too, must make difficult lifestyle changes. Stopping our chemical use will not be enough. Chapter 5 will help us analyze our living situations, recovery support programs, jobs and daily activities, and relationships in order to build a more stable lifestyle for recovery. We'll also identify specific areas that may threaten our recovery.

Identifying High-Risk Situations

Identifying situations that endanger our sobriety is particularly important. Emotions and thinking in early recovery are strained. We may not always make the most rational choices. We can easily place ourselves in high-risk situations.

Example 12. Lori had been caught with drugs and charged with possession of cocaine. The court had sentenced her to a drug treatment program. While there, she began to see how drugs had taken over her life. She wondered how she could possibly maintain sobriety when her live-in boyfriend was a drug dealer. Much of her life centered on their relationship. He was her only means of support. She questioned how supportive her boyfriend would be of her recovery.

Some of us are on a "recovery" or "treatment" high. We're caught up in the excitement of starting a new life and forget that we do not yet possess the skills and knowledge to cope with high-risk situations.

[see example 13]

Wendy had never considered that her workplace might be a high-risk situation for her. She had no concrete plan for how she would stay sober when she returned to work. How would she deal with severe urges to use drugs and alcohol again? She assumed that her knowledge of her addiction would keep her out of danger. Wendy was unprepared to cope with a workplace where drug and alcohol use is common.

Not recognizing high-risk situations is often a factor in a return to chemical use. We'll identify our high-risk situations in chapter 6.

Coping with Using Urges

When we first stop our chemical use, we're highly susceptible to using urges. Sometimes the urges can be especially powerful. We can develop skills and specific plans to cope with these situations.

Preparing a concrete plan to handle urges gives us a tool to use when we unexpectedly encounter thoughts about drug or alcohol use. An old saying goes, "If you feel like drinking, call your recovery sponsor." In reality, if we feel like drinking, we call the liquor store. Preparation is essential. We'll learn how to cope with using urges in chapter 7.

Coping with Emotions

In the process of our recovery, we may find ourselves undergoing emotional turmoil or feeling overwhelmed. Anger, fear, resentments, shame, and grief are common reactions to other people, places, and things. We still possess irrational thinking and behavior. We find that the destructive behaviors of our past have traumatized us and our families, friends, and co-workers.

Many of us used chemicals to escape from our emotions. Our emotional growth stopped when our chemical use started. Our chemicals became an escape from reality—a stopping of our personal development. We escaped real-life experiences that would have helped us form coping skills. Our emotional issues may be beyond our coping skills at this time and can easily lead us back to chemical use.

PERSONAL STORIES

Example 13. Wendy works as a waitress in a popular bar. Before entering treatment, she had spent most of her time with other employees after hours using drugs and alcohol. Her substance abuse counselor has questioned her about staying in this working environment now that she has chosen sobriety.

We need a way to process our emotions and a philosophy to guide us through this time. This is a particularly important part of the recovery process.

Chapters 8 and 9 explore irrational thinking and how emotions affect us. We'll look at simple ways to cope with our emotions and change our thinking and behavior.

Avoiding Issues

Compulsive activities—such as gambling, working long hours, jumping into relationships, or staying overly busy—keep us from paying attention to the real issues in our lives: ourselves and our self-defeating attitudes and behaviors. We may find that we're acting "crazy" or obsessing over other people, places, or things. Rather than deal with our emotions and problems, we unconsciously focus on other activities. Then we don't have to deal with our emotional pain.

We may also choose to withdraw or isolate ourselves from others to avoid people or issues we find uncomfortable. We stop our interactions with our recovery support system or tell everyone we're fine. This isolation and withdrawal from help is dangerous. We need to remember the saying, "My head is a dangerous neighborhood to be in alone."

Without contact with others, we tend to lose our sense of reality. We may construct beliefs that are untrue and that lead us back to chemical use. We tell ourselves we're all right when we're not.

We must start to build intimate social relationships with other recovering people. We need to let people know what's really going on with us. Just going to support meetings or interacting superficially with other people won't work.

Chapter 10 will help us identify the dangers of compulsive behavior, isolation, and withdrawal.

Spiritual Development

As we progress on our journey into recovery, we discover that we don't hold all the answers. We're not in control. We realize that for lasting recovery we need to turn to some type of Higher Power for help.

For some of us, our Higher Power may be God. Some of us ask for help from people who are wiser than we. People with more knowledge become our Higher Power.

Whatever form our Higher Power takes, we need to develop a concept of who we are and how we relate to our Higher Power, others, and the world. Chapter 11 will help us to explore our own spiritual concepts and to develop an attitude of gratitude and acceptance—essentials for recovery.

Integration into Recovery

Our goal is to integrate the principles of recovery into our everyday lives. In this way, our program of abstinence from alcohol and other drugs simply becomes part of our normal living routine and a means for personal growth. We realize that without an active, ongoing plan for abstinence and personal growth, we'll slide back into the "old habits and thinking."

By developing coping skills and a stable foundation, we have started the process of making our lifestyle fit our recovery. This base provides the stabilization we need to move on to further stabilization and development. We achieve the serenity that we've been searching for.

Remember:

- We should never underestimate the power of our addiction.
- It is essential to build a firm foundation to handle the ups and downs of early recovery.
- Our goal is making our lifestyle fit our recovery, not making our recovery fit our lifestyle.
- We need to resist I-can-do-it-myself thinking. Asking for help can provide answers and comfort.
- We can use others as a resource and for measuring our progress in recovery.
- The HOW principle—being Honest, Open, and Willing—can help us develop a healthy recovery attitude.
- We need to be patient in our recovery and not go too fast.
- We need to develop a spiritual nature.
- *Life was not meant to be free of emotional pain.*

Keeping sober is the most important thing in my life. The most important decision I ever made was my decision to give up drinking. I am convinced that my whole life depends on not taking that first drink. Nothing in the world is as important to me as my own sobriety. Everything I have, my whole life, depends on that one thing.

Twenty-Four Hours a Day
January 6

NOTES

Chapter 5

Building a Stable Foundation for Recovery

 nce we've stopped using chemicals, we're faced with the real stumbling block. That block is accepting that we need to make many other significant changes in our lives. We go from a lifestyle that encourages chemical use to one that promotes sobriety. At this point in our recovery, we're particularly vulnerable to falling back into chemical use. With a stable lifestyle, we increase our chances of avoiding a relapse.

Making lifestyle changes requires courage. We must be truthful and willing to make and act on difficult decisions; we need to confront our greatest fears. If we give in to our fears, we find ourselves minimizing or denying our true circumstances.

Example 14. Jan was attending an outpatient treatment program for her drug use. The counselor asked about her living situation. Jan said that both her roommates drank and drugged heavily. There was a party almost every night. Jan admitted her social life revolved around the parties in her apartment. Jan realized that she had no support for her recovery where she was living. Her chances of remaining sober in that environment were small.

Example 15. Denny drank at home alone. He knew that people who tried to return to their old drinking places didn't do well in recovery. Then he realized that his solitary existence in his apartment was his "bar." He doubted that he could remain in that environment and stay sober.

Example 16. Julie lived with her boyfriend. Their relationship revolved around the use of chemicals. He supplied the drugs and alcohol and used that to control the relationship. He was against Julie's attending a treatment program. He did not want to deal with a woman who was learning to be independent and no longer controlled by chemicals. Julie hoped that he would be supportive but soon found that he was trying to sabotage her recovery.

We can establish a firm foundation for recovery by identifying strengths and weaknesses in four basic lifestyle areas:

1. Living situation
2. Recovery support system
3. Job or daily activities
4. Relationships

Stable Living Situation

Without a supportive and stable living situation, we have little chance of maintaining abstinence. Establishing a living situation that helps our recovery involves examining the setting: the location, the potential for chemical use, and the people in the setting.

☞ *[see examples 14, 15, and 16]*

How will your present living situation affect your recovery? Take time to examine positives and negatives of the circumstances in your home. Ask yourself the following questions.

1. How does my current living situation support my recovery?

   _____

2. Do I live with someone who uses chemicals?_____

   _____

3. Are there alcohol or other drugs in my home?_____

   _____

4. Do I live alone? Did I use at home? _____

   _____

5. Do the people I live with respect my decision to be in recovery?

   _____

6. Is the neighborhood I live in helpful or harmful to my recovery?

   _____

Use your answers to the questions to list the positives and negatives about your present living situation. Ask family members, friends, or your recovery support team to help you. Remember that they may see benefits or dangers that you can't. They can also help you answer questions or discuss concerns.

Recovery is difficult under the best of conditions.

How my present living situation works with my recovery:

_____

_____

_____

_____

How my present living situation works against my recovery:

_____

_____

_____

_____

Review the list of how your current situation works against your recovery. Are there situations you will need to change? (Note: You may be tempted to say, "Yes, that could be a problem, but I'll be able to handle it." Be aware that part of you will want to play down the severity of your addiction to avoid uncomfortable changes.)

Identify two areas of your living situation that you need to change:

1. _____

_____

_____

_____

2. _____

_____

_____

_____

Now that you've identified situations that work against your recovery, make an *action plan* to deal with these situations. Write answers to the following questions.

Stability = Improving our chances of staying sober

1. What actions do you need to take? (Be prepared with a step-by-step, concrete plan.)

   _____

   _____

   _____

   _____

   _____

   _____

   _____

2. What will be the hardest part for you to do? _____

   _____

   _____

   _____

   _____

   _____

3. Whom will you need to help you? (Remember: You don't have to do everything yourself.)

   _____

   _____

   _____

4. When can you start your plan? (Don't procrastinate.)

   _____

5. Discuss this plan with a counselor and other people in recovery.

Stable Recovery Support System

How many hours a week did you spend being preoccupied with drugs and alcohol, using or coming down, and being hung over? Be honest. Don't minimize. Write that number here: 👉	_____ hours per week.
How many hours a week do you plan on devoting to your recovery? Write that number here: 👉	_____ hours per week.

Is there a substantial difference between the two numbers? If it's true that your life has been conditioned by your using thinking and behavior, can you realistically make a change with the figure you've calculated? For most of us, the answer is no. Recovery from drugs and alcohol requires an intense, ongoing effort.

❖❖❖

If we could have achieved recovery by ourselves, we probably wouldn't be reading this book. A principle behind recovery is that together we can accomplish something that we could not do alone. This means that we must take the time to turn to others for advice and guidance.

[see examples 17 and 18] 👉

The more recovery-related people, places, and things we surround ourselves with, the easier our path becomes. We need to look closely at how we can establish an effective recovery support system.

For many of us, this book may be our first and only contact with the concept of recovery; the book itself may be our only support at this point. Others of us will have a treatment program counselor, an employee assistance person, or a therapist to guide us. We may have already been in a recovery program but somehow lost our stability along the way. For some of us, our first formal experience with recovery may be through a Twelve Step or other self-help program.

Example 17. Phil believed that because he knew he was an alcoholic and addict, he could maintain sobriety on his own. He resisted suggestions from professionals and friends to develop a sound support system. In a short time, he was back to chemical use. He forgot that if he could have accomplished sobriety by himself, he would have done so long ago. Phil was trying the same thing over and over but expecting different results.

Example 18. Kelly had gone to Twelve Step meetings for a long period. She finally quit going when she still couldn't maintain abstinence. She tried several other groups but had the same result. Kelly's problem was not in the different groups she tried but rather in the fact that she resisted becoming involved with the people she encountered.

EXERCISE 5c

Assess your assets and liabilities for building a support system. Ask yourself the following questions.

	YES	NO

1. Do I already have a sponsor, home group, or friends in recovery?

2. Do I have a supportive recovery group and people whom I haven't relied on?

3. Have I ever had problems establishing a stable recovery support system?

   If yes, what got in the way? What would get in the way of building a solid recovery program now?

   _____

   _____

4. Have I had experience with a self-help group such as Alcoholics Anonymous, Narcotics Anonymous, Rational Recovery, or Women for Sobriety?

   If yes, how did this work for me? Did I take the group seriously, or did I lack commitment?

   _____

   _____

5. What personal characteristics could stop me from reaching out to others for help?

   _____

   _____

6. Is there a part of me that still insists I should be able to do this by myself?

7. Am I trying the same thing over and over again but expecting different results?

Use your answers to the questions to list the positives and negatives about your situation. Again, ask others to help you see benefits or dangers that may not be apparent to you.

Assets for building my recovery system:

_____

_____

_____

_____

Liabilities for building my recovery system:

_____

_____

_____

_____

Identify two areas that you will need to change in building a stable recovery support system:

1. _____

_____

_____

_____

2. _____

_____

_____

_____

Now that you've identified liabilities in constructing a stable recovery support system, make an *action plan* to deal with these liabilities. Write answers to the following questions.

1. What actions do you need to take? (Be prepared with a step-by-step, concrete plan.)

_____

_____

_____

_____

_____

_____

2. What will be the hardest part for you to do? _____

_____

_____

_____

_____

3. Whom will you need to help you? (Remember: You don't have to do everything yourself.)

_____

_____

_____

4. When can you start your plan? (Don't procrastinate.)

_____

5. Discuss this plan with a counselor and other people in recovery.

Conditioned behaviors and thinking are difficult to change. We must set our course and be patient. We need to surround ourselves with people who understand and support our recovery. As we develop a stable recovery support system, we find that the emotional ups and downs of our lives are less frequent. By sharing with other recovering people, we construct a "pressure relief valve."

Stable Job or Daily Activities

In early recovery, structure and stability are needed on a daily basis. Those of us new to recovery frequently lack daily disciplines. When we have too much time on our hands, we risk filling it with using thoughts and behaviors. We need to remember that, when triggered, our limbic systems can quickly provide those old thoughts and feelings.

We need to feel good about our accomplishments on a daily basis. We build self-esteem by doing esteemable things.

 **EXERCISE 5d**

How would you handle the following situations?

After finishing an inpatient addiction program, Saul returned to work in a construction field where drug and alcohol use was extensive both on the job and after work. To be part of the team, Saul felt he needed to be present during these using activities. Saul found that, when he included himself in these activities, he had severe using urges and felt out of place. He knew he was putting himself in a dangerous situation.

Things I did today:
1) Got up
2) Went to work
3) Interacted with others
4) Stayed sober

What would you do if you had Saul's problem?

_____

_____

_____

_____

_____

_____

Before going through treatment, Gwen started drinking when her children left for school. She isolated herself from others so that she could devote her day to her drinking. Now that she is trying to stay sober, she finds herself alone at home, bored and wishing that she could drink just to relieve her boredom. It has become clear to Gwen that she needs structured daily activities to help her resist using urges.

What are some options for Gwen?

_____

_____

_____

_____

_____

EXERCISE 5e

What is your job or daily life situation like? Ask yourself the following questions.

	YES	NO
1. Do I have daily structured activities?		
2. Do I work with people who use?		
3. Does my daily schedule or working environment support recovery?		
5. Am I in a high-stress environment? Do family, employer, or personal expectations increase my stress level?		

Use your answers to the questions to list the assets and liabilities of your daily schedule.

Assets for recovery in my job or daily activities:

_____

_____

_____

_____

Situations dangerous to my sobriety in my job or daily activities:

_____

_____

_____

_____

Identify two areas that you need to change in your daily lifestyle:

1. _____

_____

_____

_____

2. _____

_____

_____

_____

Now that you've identified situations that are dangerous to your sobriety in your job or daily activities, make an *action plan* to deal with these situations. Write answers to the following questions.

1. What actions do you need to take? (Be prepared with a step-by-step, concrete plan.)

   _____

   _____

   _____

   _____

   _____

   _____

   _____

   _____

2. What will be the hardest part for you to do? _____

   _____

   _____

   _____

   _____

   _____

3. Whom will you need to help you? (Remember: You don't have to do everything yourself.)

   _____

   _____

   _____

4. When can you start your plan? (Don't procrastinate.)

   _____

5. Discuss this plan with a counselor and other people in recovery.

It's easy to brush aside dangers in the workplace or in daily routines. We can tell ourselves that we'll be strong enough to handle them. But we need to avoid taking chances and plan for possible dangers. Staying busy in structured activities keeps our minds from dwelling on our problems. Now is not the time to try to make up for lost time with our families or in our jobs. We're seeking moderation in our lives.

Stable Relationships

Many of us have damaged our relationships with friends and family. They may have pulled away from us as our addiction became worse. Some of the relationships we've held on to may not be helpful or stable. They can create excess stress through irrational expectations or a long history of resentments.

We need the stability of healthy relationships to help us through early recovery. We must identify relationships that may be harmful to us. Some of these harmful relationships are with people from whom we desperately seek approval.

[see example 19] 👉

Max has forgotten that the development of trust takes time. Because of his past history, his family has every right not to trust him. Max's continued efforts to repair this relationship have only driven his family and him further apart and have caused enough resentment to jeopardize his recovery.

[see example 20] 👉

Why do they act like there's something WRONG with me?

PERSONAL STORIES

Example 19. *Max has been through chemical dependency treatment seven times. His family members have endured much emotional suffering. They have become fearful for his life and frustrated by his inability to attain sobriety. They informed him they could no longer keep in contact with him while he is using. Max now has three months of sobriety and would like to reunite with his family. He has become angry that they do not yet trust him. He resents what he sees as their rejection of him.*

Example 20. *Most of Sherry's friends and family say they support her recovery. She feels comfortable that they would not do anything to harm her. At the first family gathering after treatment, her father offered her a beer, saying, "You can have one. Just don't get drunk." Her best friend handed her a joint, thinking she had gone to treatment for alcohol, not drugs.*

PERSONAL STORIES

Example 21. Tim's parents said they supported his recovery although his whole family drinks heavily. On Thanksgiving, Tim decided to play it safe and cele-brate with his recovering friends. He chose not to be around the heavy drinking and intoxication of his relatives. When he told his mother of his decision, she became furious. She said, "So you think that your AA friends are more important than family." Tim felt guilty after the conver-sation and somehow felt he had let down his family.

It was a mistake for Sherry to think that others understand what addiction is all about. We need to be careful of our expectations of others as well as of their expectations for us. People we think support our recovery may place us in an uncomfortable situation.

☜ *[see example 21]*

 EXERCISE 5f

Take time to think about the relationships in your life and how they will affect your recovery. Ask yourself the following questions.

1. What are my relationships with nonrecovering people like?

2. Do I have many close friends, or am I more of a "loner"?

3. Do friends and family really want to see me sober, or are they more concerned about my not being a problem to them?

4. Are my relationships built around using situations?

5. Do I feel others place too many expectations on me?

6. Do I have to live up to an image that is not really who I want to be?

List the people who will be assets to your recovery:

_____

_____

_____

List the people who may be liabilities to your recovery:

_____

_____

_____

Identify two people or situations that may be dangerous to your recovery:

1. _____

2. _____

 **Action Plan**

Now that you've identified people or situations that could be dangerous to your sobriety, make an *action plan* to deal with these people or situations. Write answers to the following questions.

1. What actions do you need to take? (Be prepared with a step-by-step, concrete plan.)

   _____

   _____

   _____

   _____

   _____

   _____

   _____

2. What will be the hardest part for you to do? _____

   _____

   _____

   _____

   _____

   _____

3. Whom will you need to help you? (Remember: You don't have to do everything yourself.)

   _____

   _____

   _____

4. When can you start your plan? (Don't procrastinate.)

   _____

5. Discuss this plan with a counselor and other people in recovery.

We rarely have complete stability in our lives when entering early recovery. What's important is to identify problem areas and to find ways to manage these situations. Sometimes that involves simple changes. In other cases, it involves making large lifestyle changes. The more stable our lives are, the more apt we are to maintain our sobriety. The more recovering people we can surround ourselves with, the easier the emotional transition will be.

Remember:

- Recovery must be based on a solid foundation: stable living situation, stable recovery support system, stable job or daily activities, and stable relationships.
- The *fewer* stabilizing factors we have in our lives, the more work we need to do.
- We need to make our lifestyle fit our recovery, not our recovery fit our lifestyle.

Chapter 6

Identifying High-Risk Situations

elapse to chemical use is especially common in early recovery. We lack a lifestyle that supports abstinence. We've had little experience at remaining sober. We haven't developed activities or coping skills to help us through situations that could threaten our sobriety. High-risk situations can be described as

1. any person, place, or situation connected with using drugs or alcohol

2. any time we're around alcohol or drugs

3. any place or situation that is associated with high stress

Example 22. John had finished an outpatient substance abuse program. In the past, he spent his leisure time at a local sports bar with his friends. He understood that this could be a problem but thought that he was strong enough to handle it. Besides, his friends knew that he'd quit drinking and drugging. It felt very comfortable to him to return to his old hangout. The smell, the noise, the people, the atmosphere were all the same. He found that the only thing missing was a drink. One of his friends offered to buy him a beer, saying, "Just have one, man, you're not an alcoholic. You just did too many drugs." The next morning, John called in sick to work. He still had some drugs left from the night before, and he was planning another trip to the liquor store. He was immediately back into his addiction.

As recovering people, we're faced with deciding how to avoid high-risk situations on a daily basis. Some of these will be easy decisions. We'll probably choose *not* to attend the "Let's Get Acquainted, All You Can Drink or Use for $5 Block Party" being sponsored by the local liquor distributor and the friendly representatives of a Colombian drug cartel. But what about situations involving family, friends, or job responsibilities? Is there danger in these seemingly safe situations?

Many people return to chemical use in situations where they believe they are safe. We try to be attentive to high-risk circumstances. It's unlikely that we would knowingly put ourselves in a position that would lead us back to chemical use. The problem is that we're usually not aware of what actually makes up a high-risk situation. This lack of awareness can be dangerous.

Defining High-Risk Situations

Three simple criteria can guide us in recognizing threats to our sobriety.

1. *Any person, place, or situation connected with using drugs or alcohol.* For some of us, this includes just about everywhere. We know that using friends or using situations can bring on urges, some of which can be severe. This phenomenon is unpredictable. If we're in a place where we've used before, we can never be sure that we won't be overwhelmed by sudden urges. Old thoughts and emotions can come back in a moment. Our brains have many automatic, unhealthy responses just waiting to be triggered.

[see example 22]

John thought he would be able to handle using urges. He knew he was dependent on drugs and alcohol but believed he would be "strong enough to handle it." He assumed his friends would support his recovery.

When we rely on logic and willpower to handle our chemical use, we dismiss the power and unpredictability of our addiction. We can't depend on nonrecovering people to understand what we need. They haven't experienced addiction. They most likely don't understand addiction or the lengths that we need to go to remain sober.

2. *Any time we're around alcohol or drugs.* Be cautious. If drugs and alcohol are around, there's always a chance that we could use them *even if we firmly believe we won't.* We can't predict how we'll react in the presence of chemicals.

[see example 23] 👉

Our ability to resist drugs and alcohol is unpredictable. *The belief that "I don't feel like using so I'm okay" is just not valid!* We can't judge our commitment to sobriety based on what we're thinking or feeling at any given moment. Dana's experience shows that past triggers can change our thinking in seconds. When we encounter situations where chemicals are present, we must exercise caution.

3. *Any place or situation that is associated with high stress.* Some of us forget that stress builds up. Rather than being triggered by a single catastrophic event, stress may result from a number of different areas in our lives. Poor financial conditions, relationships, and work situations can build collectively to create an overwhelming level of stress.

Stress plays an important role in our ability to handle high-risk situations. When overly stressed, we tend to make irrational decisions. We want to relieve the stress as quickly as possible. If the stress becomes too intense, we may choose to use chemicals to cope with the discomfort.

[see example 24] 👉

Carolyn had placed herself in an extremely stressful situation without having thought about the possible consequences. Any place that has the potential for "bad news"—such as a doctor appointment, a court proceeding, or a meeting with someone who has "pushed our buttons" in the past—can be a problem. We do not yet have the skills to handle high-stress situations safely.

Avoiding people or places that have caused or could cause emotional trauma is also important. Attending a funeral, visiting a cemetery, interacting with former lovers, and confronting past failures all have the ability to trigger traumatic memories. These emotions can create using urges to suppress the resulting emotional hurt. We revert to old thinking and behaviors to deal with the pain.

PERSONAL STORIES

Example 23. Dana had six months of abstinence from drugs. His company was having a holiday party, and he felt obligated to go. He knew that there would be alcohol in the restaurant, but Dana reasoned that he was a heroin addict and seldom had any desire for alcohol. He felt safe in his decision to attend this function. For the first two hours, Dana had a wonderful time with no using urges. Then, Dana's ex-wife came in with another man. Within seconds, the old resentments and anger were back, and all he could think about was having a drink. He left immediately but was baffled by the idea that when his old emotions were triggered, he sought help from whatever chemical was around, not just his chemical of choice. He was amazed at how fast his thinking changed. It had taken only a few seconds.

Example 24. Carolyn went to her physician for the results of her biopsy. As she sat in the waiting room, her fear was mounting. She had never experienced this type of anxiety without reducing it with chemicals. She thought that if the results showed cancer, she deserved a drink. If she didn't have cancer, it seemed right to celebrate.

Looking for Solutions

In each of the previous examples, people put themselves in a high-risk situation without realizing or preparing for it. Some of us may think we can't go anywhere without risking our sobriety! Remember that we're focusing on identification. If recovering alcoholics and addicts frequently relapse in situations where they are unaware and unprepared, then it's important for us to be able to identify dangerous situations. This gives us choices.

One choice we always have is to not put ourselves in a high-risk situation. If we're undecided, we can turn to others in recovery for guidance. We may not see potentially dangerous situations ourselves.

If we determine that we cannot avoid a high-risk situation, we can take the following steps:

1. *We can take someone with us who is in recovery or who understands addiction.* We need support in a high-risk situation. Most people are not knowledgeable about addiction. We may hear them say, "I know you went to treatment. Here, have a beer. Just don't get drunk." Many times people who know about our dependency will choose *not* to intervene even when they see us using for fear of saying or doing the wrong thing. Having someone who understands us and our fears and urges is important. It keeps us accountable.

2. *We can give ourselves permission to leave an uncomfortable situation.* We don't need to test ourselves in the presence of drugs or alcohol. We've taken that test before and failed. Sometimes an event that we believe will be relatively safe can turn on us. This is the unpredictable part of our addiction. We can give ourselves permission to leave before we attend an event.

👉 [see example 25]

Letting others know ahead of time that we may choose to leave makes it easier for us to make that decision later. We won't feel as though we're letting others down. Remember that our recovery comes first. It's far more important than any approval we may get by staying in a dangerous situation.

Example 25. Jean and Bill attended a social function for Bill's company. Jean told Bill before the event that she had concerns about how she might react to the liquor that was sure to be there. They discussed this and decided they would drive separately so Jean could leave if she needed to.

3. *We can have a reliable way to leave should we choose to do so.*
   When we give ourselves permission to leave an uncomfortable
   situation, we need a reliable way to leave. Some of us may not
   have driving privileges as a consequence of our chemical use,
   but we can avoid being "trapped" at an event with no way to
   leave. We can plan beforehand to have a sponsor or friend pick
   us up.

How would you have handled the situations of John, Dana, and
Carolyn? What would you have done in their positions to protect
yourself?

John

_____

_____

_____

_____

Dana

_____

_____

_____

_____

Carolyn

_____

_____

_____

_____

Make a plan for yourself by answering the following questions.

What are some of the high-risk situations you know you will encounter?

_____

_____

_____

How will you manage those situations?

_____

_____

_____

Whom can you go to for help in identifying and preparing for high-risk situations?

_____

_____

_____

Remember:

- In early recovery, we're more susceptible to a return to chemical use than we may think.
- To protect ourselves, we need to constantly monitor ourselves.
- What we seek is *awareness*. If we're aware of risky situations, we can act to keep safe.
- We need to be cautious around drugs and alcohol.
- We can't assume that knowing we're addicted will keep us sober.
- We can't judge how well we're doing by whether we have using urges.
- We can give ourselves permission to leave uncomfortable situations.
- Phrases such as "I think I'm *strong* enough to handle that situation" or "I'll be okay. I know I can't drink" are red flags that our thinking is offtrack. We're in trouble when we think we've got this recovery thing under control.
- In time, preventive thinking becomes automatic.

Chapter 7
Coping with Using Urges

n urge or craving to use alcohol or other drugs is a normal physical and emotional reaction to stopping alcohol and other drug use. Our bodies and minds have adapted to receiving a regular supply of chemicals. When we stop taking our chemicals, our bodies and minds still want them.

When we have a craving, we may experience physical symptoms. Our hearts may beat faster or we may salivate when watching a beer commercial. We can encounter cravings without warning or by some trigger, such as seeing our drug of choice or driving past our dealer's house.

When we stop our chemical use, urges to use our drugs can be frequent and intense. As we focus on developing a lifestyle free of alcohol and other drugs and based on personal growth, cravings become fewer and farther between but can still occur.

Most urges are short-lived and last no longer than a few minutes. This means that easy access to drugs or alcohol can be dangerous. It only takes a moment to walk to the refrigerator, open a beer, and start to drink again. With an impulsive act, our dependency has been reignited, and we find ourselves deeply into our addiction again. But, if we don't have drugs or alcohol nearby, the urge may pass before we can get to the liquor store or have a chance to contact our drug dealer.

Careful planning is the key. If we have a plan outlining how we'll handle these situations, we can save our recovery.

How Could I Talk Myself into Using Again?

When life becomes stressful or if something triggers our emotions and memories, we may return to chemical use. *Euphoric recall* and *magical thinking* are methods we use to rationalize, or excuse, a return to using.

Euphoric Recall

Euphoric recall refers to "romancing" our past use.

> ***Example:*** *"It sure was great at Bob's party that night. I really got wasted. Gosh, those were great days. I sure haven't had that much fun since I stopped drugging. Sobriety is boring."*

Euphoric recall is the process of thinking favorably about our *past* using experiences. Our memory becomes very selective. We think about how good it was to use, and we forget or minimize the consequences of our actions. We miss the excitement of the "old days."

Magical Thinking

Magical, or delusional, thinking is planning for controlled future use.

> ***Example:*** *Barbara's husband is going to be gone for a week on business. She remembers the many times she secretly drank while he was gone. She starts to plan how she could drink again and stop before he returns.*

Magical thinking is when we believe that social using or controlling our use might be an option. We question whether we're dependent on chemicals. We start to believe that we may be able to use "one more time" and then quit before suffering any consequences. We may be so caught up in the thought of using again that we forget about the past consequences of our use. We delude, or fool, ourselves into believing we can control our chemical use. We deny our powerlessness over our addiction.

Challenging Euphoric Recall and Magical Thinking

One problem in dealing with urges is mistakenly making the situation worse rather than better. If an urge lasts longer than a few minutes, we may be doing something to prolong its effect. We intensify our urges by focusing on euphoric recall or magical thinking or by putting ourselves in high-risk situations (see chapter 6) that trigger more intense thoughts.

We need to challenge euphoric recall and magical thinking immediately. Early intervention is the key. When we have an urge to use, we can take the following steps:

1. *Try to "short-circuit" the thinking by challenging the using thoughts.* Within the first ten seconds, we should think about what would happen if we were to follow through and use again. We can plan for these occasions by creating a thought sequence that describes the worst circumstance or consequence of past chemical use.

   How did we feel emotionally? Physically? What was it like to face our families? Our employers? This is called "thinking the drink or drug through" or "playing the tape through to the end." It puts us back into contact with the reality of the consequences of our use. It contradicts addictive thinking.

[see example 26] ☞

PERSONAL STORIES

Example 26. Bev had to work late again. She left the office tired and angry. A memory from her old using days flashed in her mind. She remembered that stopping by her favorite bar for a few drinks had always made her feel better. The urge was so strong she could taste the drink.

Bev knew how to handle the urge. She carried a card in her purse that described what happened the last time she had a drink. She read through it and remembered that the last time she'd gone to that bar, she lost control of her drinking and ended up in jail for DUI. She thought of how embarrassed she was when her mother had to bail her out. Bev didn't want her name in the paper again. She decided to go home.

Thinking can be our biggest obstacle to recovery.

2. *Remove ourselves from any person, place, or situation that may have triggered the using thoughts.* We can know what our triggers are! We don't have to be afraid to leave an uncomfortable situation. We can't be concerned about what others may think. Our sobriety comes first.

3. *Contact someone and talk about how we're feeling.* Using thoughts are normal and not a sign of weakness. Calling someone and talking about what we've encountered can relax/dilute/ soften or end the urge. Other people with chemical dependency have been there and know exactly what we're experiencing. They know that we're not weak. They understand the need for talking about these intense feelings.

The object is to *lessen* the severity of the urge so that we can cope with it. It may not go away completely. If it reoccurs, we need to relax, start at the beginning, and calmly challenge the thought again.

1. To challenge euphoric recall, or positive using memories from the past, create a specific thought sequence about specific past events. Describe the most severe consequences of your past use. This includes events, devastating feelings, people you hurt, legal problems, or relationship issues. When challenging euphoric recall, you need to be completely honest. Write down what *really* happened when you used.

2. Magical thinking says that you could use one more time—that you could somehow control your chemical use. When you start to have this type of thinking, consider how using again would play out *in reality*. You might imagine that using again would be okay, but what would *really* happen? Think the drink or drug through or play the tape through to the end. Write down a sequence of what would happen if you started to use again.

First, I would

_____

_____

_____

_____

What would happen next?

_____

_____

_____

_____

What would happen next?

_____

_____

_____

_____

And next?

_____

_____

_____

_____

When we start to think about using, we can play out the sequence of what has happened in the past and what would happen in the future. We need to live in the honesty and reality of what our lives were like when we used chemicals.

Example 27. Jane jumped up out of a sound sleep. She dreamed that she had returned to using drugs. The excitement of the using and yet the shame about her failure to stay sober were intense. Now that she was awake, she wondered whether it was actually a dream. It seemed so real.

Using Dreams

Just as we have dreams about different aspects of our lives, we also may dream about using chemicals again. The disturbing thing about the using dream is the reality of it. We snap back to consciousness startled and shaken. Many times, we believe that the dream was real and that we've somehow lost our sobriety. Because they seem so real, these experiences can be frightening, even for someone with a long period of sobriety.

👉 *[see example 27]*

The using dream shows us what's going on in our heads. When awake, we're aware of the possibility of using thoughts and can cope with them. When asleep, these dreams become powerful messengers of the strength of our dependency, our feelings of shame or powerlessness, or our fears about relapsing to chemical use. It is helpful to realize that using dreams are common and not necessarily a sign that we will relapse.

Remember:

- Urges will be brief unless we do something to prolong them. We can talk to others and challenge the thinking immediately.
- Using thoughts and dreams become less frequent with time. We need to be patient.
- Urges and using dreams do not necessarily mean we're doing something wrong in our recovery.
- Using dreams and urges to use chemicals are normal. They are part of the mind-set of the person with chemical dependency.

Chapter 8
Exploring Emotions

As we work through the stages of early recovery, we face a large roadblock—our inability to effectively deal with our emotions. We used chemicals for years to escape from or to cushion our feelings. When we stopped feeling, we also stopped growing emotionally.

Without our chemicals, we begin to "feel" the emotions we previously buried. Although this is a step in the right direction, it can be difficult and painful. Because we stopped growing emotionally, we didn't develop the skills to cope with our newly found feelings.

In the past, our inability to handle painful or intense feelings led us to drink or drug. We lived the credo of the alcoholic and addict: "I should never be uncomfortable, physically or emotionally. If I am, I must end it with all due haste." When we felt overwhelmed and out of control, we believed we had the right to drink and drug to feel better. It was easy to avoid taking responsibility for our feelings and actions.

To remain in recovery, we must explore our emotions and learn coping skills. At first, the intensity and diversity of our emotions can overwhelm us. We may feel too much and overreact, or we may numb ourselves and feel little or nothing. Some of us discover that we can't identify our feelings. We find ourselves uncomfortable emotionally but are not sure why. To manage feelings effectively, we first need to identify what they are.

Identifying Feelings

Identifying feelings can be difficult because feelings are nonverbal, or unspoken, experiences. Those of us in recovery have additional difficulty because we've numbed our internal experiences for years by using chemicals. The inability to identify our feelings or the tendency to minimize our feelings leads to increased stress and a return to chemical use.

Refer to the "I am feeling..." chart on the next page for help in completing this exercise on identifying your feelings.

1. Look over the list to find words that describe how you're feeling *now*. Remember that you can have more than one feeling at a time.

   _____

2. Think back over the past week. Was there a time that you were especially emotional? Find those feelings and write them here.

   _____

3. Is there *one* feeling that you experience frequently? Find it and write it here.

   _____

4. Is there *one* feeling that you would like to feel less often? Find it and write it here.

   _____

I am feeling . . .		
Afraid	Giving	Pessimistic
Amused	Glad	Pitiful
Angry	Grateful	Proud
Annoyed	Grief stricken	Rageful
Betrayed	Guilty	Regretful
Caring	Happy	Resentful
Competent	Hesitant	Revengeful
Complete	Hopeful	Sad
Confident	Hostile	Scared
Delighted	Hurt	Shameful
Dependent	Immobilized	Strong
Despairing	Impatient	Sympathetic
Discounted	Inadequate	Tender
Discouraged	Irritated	Trusting
Disgusted	Isolated	Untrusting
Distant	Jealous	Unwanted
Eager	Joyful	Useless
Encouraged	Lonely	Vulnerable
Envious	Loving	Wanted
Excited	Mad	Warm
Fearful	Optimistic	Wary
Frightened	Overwhelmed	Weak
Fulfilled	Patient	

Try to limit the use of the following words. They let us be too general in identifying our feelings. We make better progress by being more specific.

Words to avoid . . .		
Bad	Depressed	Uncomfortable
Comfortable	Frustrated	Upset
Confused	Good, Fine, Great	

Owning Our Feelings

An important part of exploring feelings is learning to take responsibility for them. It's easy to blame others for how we feel. By blaming someone else, we avoid looking at our part in the problem. We hear this in our everyday conversations.

"My boss makes me angry."

"My wife/husband makes me feel inadequate."

"Those kids are driving me crazy."

Our belief that others are responsible for our problems and feelings gives away our power to change. When we place the power for our happiness on someone or something that we have no control over, we condemn ourselves to feeling helpless, hurt, and resentful. Until that person changes, we can't be happy. Since it's unlikely that the person will change, we stay stuck.

We learn that we have the power to change how we feel. We have choices about how we react to others. Making these choices demands rigorous honesty; blaming others is no longer an option we can afford. *We're responsible for our own feelings and reactions. Being responsible empowers us to make changes.*

How we respond emotionally to a person, place, or thing is based on what we believe about that person, place, or thing.

☞ *[see example 28]*

Bob and Tom both saw the *same* event—a speech. They had *entirely different* emotional reactions based on what they believed. Their belief systems determined their emotional reaction to the speech.

We can further grasp this concept by using Rational Emotive Behavior Therapy, or REBT. Rational Emotive Behavior Therapy, introduced by Albert Ellis, focuses on identifying our beliefs, empowering change, and improving our ability to cope with feelings. REBT says that when an action or event happens, we interpret it based on our thoughts, beliefs, or expectations about that event. Our interpretation of that event leads to an emotional response. The resulting emotional response can determine our behavior. We can work to identify and challenge deeply embedded and damaging irrational beliefs.

Example 28. *Bob and Tom are watching an influential Democratic politician make a speech. Bob, who is a Republican, says, "Hey! This guy is a real jerk." He's angry and disgusted about what he hears. Tom, who is a Democrat, says, "I like what he's saying. He's right about this." Tom's pleased that this person shares his beliefs.*

Each of us has a belief system. A belief system consists of our thoughts and attitudes that give meaning to the events in our lives. It involves past experiences and learning. It's our thoughts, our interpretation of our experiences, our learned values, and our expectations of ourselves and other people, places, and situations.

Some of our beliefs are rational and appropriate and some are not. It's possible that our beliefs about a particular person or event are wrong. Being human means making mistakes. Over time, we create illogical patterns of thinking that from our viewpoint seem reasonable. We come to believe that our perception is accurate. Continuing to believe these irrational thoughts leads to self-defeating thinking and behavior. Irrational beliefs can be self-talk statements such as:

I must always . . .

They should never . . .

It's *terrible* when . . .

These exaggerated, rigid, and judgmental statements form the basis of irrational, self-defeating thinking and behavior. We become stuck in all-or-nothing patterns of thought. We judge other people, places, and things by standards that don't reflect reality. Acting on false beliefs creates mistakes and confusion. We perceive that we've acted correctly but have been unjustly criticized. We become angry when others don't follow our distorted beliefs. It never occurs to us that we may be wrong.

We need a way to determine what our belief system is telling us. Is our belief and resulting feeling rational, or is it a self-defeating belief that causes us emotional distress? We can set up a simple diagram to analyze our beliefs.

Event

Thoughts and Beliefs

Emotional Response

Behavior

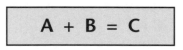

$$A + B = C$$

- **A** is any **A**ction or event we encounter. We experience life events on a daily basis that involve people, places, and situations.

- **B** is what our **B**elief system tells us. It involves our thoughts, values, and expectations about ourselves, other people, places, or situations.

- **C** is the feeling or action that results—a **C**onsequence of our belief about that person, place, or event.

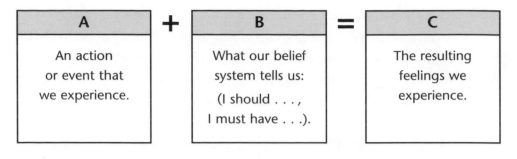

Rational Emotive Behavior Therapy shows us how to explore our feelings. It teaches us how to change our thinking and responses by altering our belief system. Our feelings are based not on the person, place, or situation but rather on what we *believe* about that person, place, or situation.

We've little control over most things in the world—traffic, other people, and unexpected frustrations—the "A" in the sequence. We do have control over our belief system—"B." We can make changes in our beliefs that will influence how we feel about things. This is an extremely important concept. *It means we have the ability to change how we feel.* We can choose not to be controlled by external situations.

[see example 29]

Example 29. Marty became angry following a driver going 45 mph in a 55 mph zone. He was already late for an appointment. He threw a cup of coffee in rage and hit the dashboard with his hand. When he arrived at his appointment, he was still resentful and made a poor presentation. He continued to be irritable for the rest of the day. Hours later, he was still angry with the slow driver. Marty had effectively ruined his day over an insignificant event.

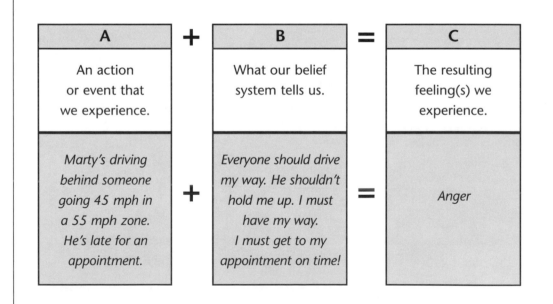

What were Marty's irrational beliefs here? The "shoulds," "musts," "it's awful," "it's terrible," "I can't"?

1. *He should* drive for *my* convenience! *Everyone should* drive *my* way.

2. *Why me? He shouldn't* hold me up!

3. *I must* have my way. *I must never* be inconvenienced.

4. *I must* get to my appointment on time! (Or, I'm no good. . . . My day will be ruined. . . . It will be terrible.)

We can see how Marty, through irrational and rigid thinking, saw the situation as being extremely disagreeable. He had no control over how the other person was driving, but he did have a choice in how to react to it.

Challenging Irrational Beliefs

When we identify an irrational belief, we can challenge it by asking ourselves:

- What is the evidence that this is true?
- Are our expectations reasonable or are they self-serving?

Marty could go through the following process to challenge his beliefs about the driving incident:

1. It's unreasonable to expect others to drive for *my* convenience.
2. Why me? Why *not* me? Am I so special?
3. It's foolish to expect things to always go *my* way.
4. I can make my best effort to get to my appointment. I can call ahead. Everything will work out all right.
5. I can accept that in spite of my best planning, I will sometimes be delayed.
6. I can't control others.

Example 30. Samantha's employer commented about a mistake she had made on the office inventory. She felt exposed and shameful. She quickly retreated to her office and isolated herself.

☞ *[see example 30]*

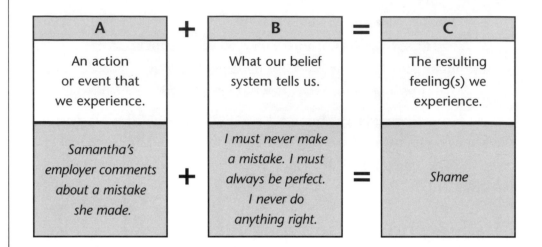

A	+	B	=	C
An action or event that we experience.	+	What our belief system tells us.	=	The resulting feeling(s) we experience.
Samantha's employer comments about a mistake she made.	+	*I must never make a mistake. I must always be perfect. I never do anything right.*	=	Shame

What beliefs would have caused Samantha to react with shame? Samantha's belief system was telling her that

1. *I must never* make a mistake.
2. *I must always* be perfect. If I make a mistake, it shows that I am worthless.
3. *I never* do anything right. There is something wrong with me.

Samantha called her recovering friends about her reaction. They were able to challenge her thinking.

 **EXERCISE 8b**

How would you challenge Samantha's statements/beliefs? Write your response on the lines below.

1. Everyone makes mistakes. A mistake does not make her worthless.

2. _____

3. _____

4. _____

If we continually question and clarify our belief system, we initiate changes in our responses. This leads to more appropriate emotional reactions to the annoyances of life. We can make changes in our emotions and behavior by

1. ceasing to focus on the offending person or situation as the cause of our discomfort
2. identifying and challenging our irrational beliefs
3. continuing to inventory our belief system for self-defeating thinking. Can we identify frequently used patterns?

Persistence is required for change. It doesn't happen overnight.

Acknowledging Feelings Based on Rational Beliefs

While some of our reactions may be based on irrational thinking, many others are based on rational thinking and sound judgment.

[see example 31] 👉

Example 31. *When Assan returned home, he found that someone had broken in and stolen his new TV and some jewelry. Assan felt angry and violated. He identified these feelings immediately. He contacted his recovery sponsor and discussed the incident.*

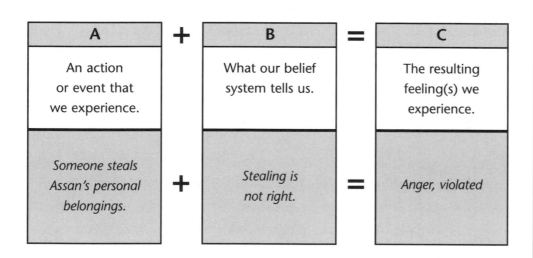

A		B		C
An action or event that we experience.	+	What our belief system tells us.	=	The resulting feeling(s) we experience.
Someone steals Assan's personal belongings.	**+**	*Stealing is not right.*	**=**	*Anger, violated*

Normally, Assan would have gone into a rage. His rage would then have led to feelings of self-pity and chemical use. Rather than let his emotions run wild, he reached out to others and used REBT to process his feelings. His rational belief was that *stealing is not right.* He chose not to fall into the irrational belief that "People *should never* steal, especially from me" or "Why did this have to happen to me?"

Assan made several conclusions.

- It *was normal* to feel some anger and violation due to his loss. He *chose* not to intensify the feelings and make the situation worse than it really was. He realized that *nothing* would be gained from rageful behavior.
- Theft is always a possibility. It's why he has insurance.
- "Why did this happen to me?" was an ego-driven statement. He remembered that a friend in recovery had said, "Why me? Why not me? Am I special that nothing bad should ever happen to me?" Assan had to conclude he was not special.
- Bad things do happen to good people.
- People do not always have control over circumstances. He knew he was powerless to change a past event.

Assan was able to turn a bad situation into one that he could cope with. He reacted rationally. He didn't blame anyone or dwell on how unfair it was. He used energy from his anger to inventory his home for other missing items and to make sure he called his insurance agent. He also thought about installing a security system. Assan believed that he could learn from this experience. He did not allow this incident to ruin his day. He did not have to resort to chemicals to feel better.

EXERCISE 8c

Pick a recent incident that resulted in a significant emotional reaction.

- In box A write down the action or event that "caused" the feelings.
- In box C write down the feeling(s) that resulted from this action.
- In box B identify the belief statement that resulted in the emotional reaction. This statement may start with: I should . . . I must . . . You should . . . You must . . . They should . . . They must . . . .

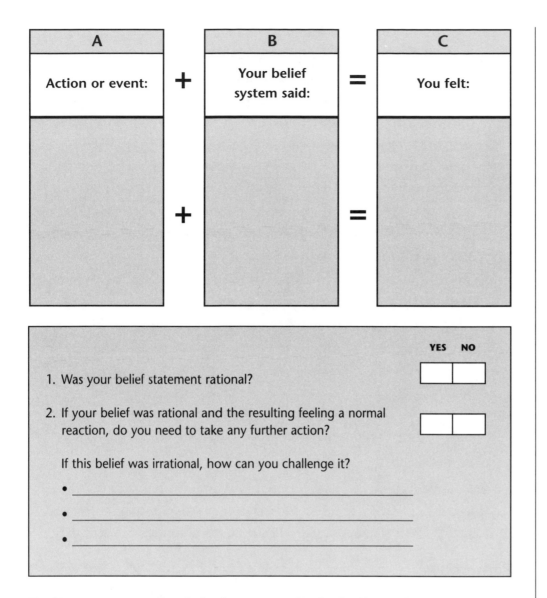

A		B		C
Action or event:	**+**	**Your belief system said:**	**=**	**You felt:**

+ **=**

	YES	NO
1. Was your belief statement rational?		
2. If your belief was rational and the resulting feeling a normal reaction, do you need to take any further action?		

If this belief was irrational, how can you challenge it?

- _____
- _____
- _____

Feelings are rooted in belief systems. To deal effectively with our emotions, we need to become skilled at identifying, analyzing, and challenging irrational beliefs.

What steps can we take to deal with intense feelings? The list below provides options.

- Abstain from using chemicals for relief.
- Get out with others. Addicts tend to isolate themselves. Recovering people can't afford to. *We need to remember that our heads are a dangerous neighborhood to be in alone.*
- Get our feelings out. We need to discuss how we feel with others. Stuffing feelings only leads to frustrations and depression.
- Listen to others. Other people in recovery have been through this. We need to get our egos out of the way and listen to what others have to say. We don't know everything.

- Don't be unique. Too often we believe that no one else could possibly understand what we're going through. Others in recovery do understand. They've been there.
- Don't take feedback personally. When others give us feedback that's hard to hear, we should take it as good direction. We need others to hold us accountable.
- Do something to help others. A good deed takes our minds off our own problems.
- Identify our issues. We can make a list of our problems. Once we've identified them, we can start looking for solutions. We can get insight or feedback from others.
- Let go. There are many things in our lives that we can't change. We can turn these over to our Higher Power.
- Meditate or pray. The more stressed we are, the more likely we are to overreact. We can learn some meditation techniques to help us relax. If we believe in the power of prayer, we can pray for the strength to endure through the stress.
- Remember that we're not alone. We should never be afraid to ask for help. *Trying to do everything ourselves keeps us stuck and frustrated.*

Our serenity and our recovery depend on our attitude. We can obtain books on REBT or other cognitive therapies at bookstores and libraries. We can make a sincere effort to build emotional stability.

Remember:

- Handling emotions appropriately is a significant part of our recovery.
- Our chemical use has limited our ability to deal with emotions and stress.
- Failure to deal with our feelings can result in stress and resentments that lead us back to chemical use.
- *Others do not determine how we feel.* We're responsible for our own feelings and actions.
- Blaming others for our feelings takes away our power to change.
- Our beliefs determine how we feel and how we react to an action or event: A+B=C.
- We can change how we react to people, places, and situations.

Chapter 9
DEALING WITH EMOTIONS

s addicts and alcoholics, we're notorious for not wanting to talk about what's bothering us. When we were using, we couldn't talk about our problems for fear someone would discover how severe our addiction was. We may have learned early in life that problems were not to be discussed openly. We may believe that to "open up" about how we feel leaves us vulnerable to manipulation or rejection by others.

Many of us used alcohol and other drugs for years to cope with the normal emotions of everyday life. It seemed that we were extremely sensitive to stress and to "bad" feelings. Whether by choice or by chance, we lacked the ability to deal with our feelings in a responsible manner.

Learning to talk about feelings is a critical part of recovery. To remain sober, we must learn the skills to deal with our emotions. Failure to do so leads us back to chemical use.

When we are troubled, we need to discuss our feelings with other people in recovery. When we share our feelings of anger, shame, or fear, we take a load off our shoulders, and we usually get some worthwhile feedback, which can be comforting, reassuring, and even inspirational.

We need to remember the saying "My head is a dangerous neighborhood to be in alone." Getting out with other people and keeping ourselves busy with positive recovery activities will leave little time for thinking about our troubles.

We may have to discuss our feelings frequently and with different people to reduce the level of anger, fear, or shame. We also need to listen to what others are saying to us. Feedback helps us see another perspective. Talking to one person about a troubling issue is seldom enough. Not everyone understands how addicts and alcoholics think.

When dealing with troublesome emotions, we need to use coping skills, communicate with others, and make changes.

Use Coping Skills

- Learn to express feelings and concerns.
- Keep realistic expectations of the world and ourselves.
- Be honest with ourselves and others. We should keep no secrets and tell no lies.
- Seek professional help. If certain emotions are disrupting our lives, a psychologist or therapist who is experienced in dealing with recovering people can help us develop the skills we need to feel better.

Communicate with Others

- Ask for help. This is crucial. We should never try to go through recovery alone. We're inexperienced with emotions. We need constructive guidance.
- Build a support system of recovering people. They have the knowledge and the experience to help.
- Set up regular meetings with people who share similar problems. A variety of self-help and recovery groups exists.

Make Changes

- Identify the problems in our lives that need to be dealt with and make the necessary changes. *We should discuss these changes with other recovering people first.* Newly recovering addicts and alcoholics frequently act without thinking things through.

- Avoid procrastination. If we get stuck, we can use others to hold us accountable for taking action.

Certain feelings seem to be a persistent problem in the early recovery period. Anger, fear, shame, and grief are the most troublesome emotions.

Anger and Resentments

Anger plays a major role in addiction. Unresolved anger, or resentment, can disrupt our lives. Yet, anger is a normal human emotion that everyone experiences. Anger is an emotional response to situations in which we feel threatened, treated unfairly, or violated.

Anger is *not* the issue. The real problem is *unresolved* anger. When we resolve our anger, we can move on.

Unresolved anger is a major cause of relapse to chemical use. We can't afford to be resentful. Resentment is the opposite of forgiveness. Resentment keeps us stuck at the point of pain. We may be filled with anger toward someone who doesn't even remember the event that made us angry or toward someone who's already died. We are the ones who suffer by holding on.

Most of us believe that other people, places, and things *make* us angry. We think that these external factors cause our feelings. We indulge ourselves in "righteous anger."

Blaming others enables us to hold on to resentments and to avoid having to change ourselves. It lets us operate from a morally superior position: I'm good, you're bad. Our work with emotions in chapter 8 taught us that our belief system is responsible for how we feel—not other people, places, and things. We can keep this in mind as we explore how we use anger.

Anger as a Positive Force

Anger can be a positive motivator. We have energy when we feel angry. Anger is part of the body's automatic survival response. Rather than yell, scream, or throw things, we can direct energy from anger into a positive action. A woman whose child died in a car accident started a national group that works to promote safer driving. Her anger produced a lifesaving organization. How can we use anger constructively?

[see example 32]

Tina was angry because she could not control her chemical use. She used that anger constructively to get help. Her anger became a lifesaving tool.

We can use our anger to make important changes. We may become angry about our job, an abusive relationship, or our lack of schooling. Our anger can energize us to make changes that will better our lives. If we are mistreated, our anger can provide the courage to assert our needs.

Anger as a Negative Force

Alcoholics and addicts look at life in a fairly self-centered way. We resent what we can't control and want life at our convenience. Many of us use anger in unhealthy ways. The following list gives reasons for and effects of our anger.

- *Anger from lack of control.* We are constantly angry with someone or something. Things never happen quickly enough. We encounter tremendous frustration when life doesn't happen according to our plan. The world seems to be against us. People in recovery refer to this way of thinking and acting as the king-baby complex: "I want what I want when I want it, and I want it now."

- *Anger as a defense.* Sometimes we intimidate others with our anger to keep them at a safe distance. Others may give in to our wishes rather than risk an angry scene. Using anger as a defense enables us to remain isolated so others don't get close enough to see all our faults. Sometimes the best defense is an angry offense.

- *Anger as a mask.* Anger can cover grief, hurt, loss, or fear. An angry exterior keeps people from finding out what we're really feeling. The other emotions are much too sensitive to deal with.

- *Being uncomfortable with feelings of anger.* We may feel that it's wrong to be angry. When we were younger, we may have been told, "Don't get angry at your baby sister" or "You keep that temper under control." These old tapes reinforce the idea that anger must be a negative thing and that we must never show we're angry. Such ideas keep us from learning to resolve anger.

- *Being overwhelmed by others' anger.* While we may have difficulty dealing with our own anger, some of us also don't know how to deal with other people's anger. We feel powerless and intimidated by other people's anger. Because we're not sure how to handle it, we quickly withdraw or avoid situations where we might encounter it. We would rather lose out on something than chance someone getting angry with us. We feel powerless, manipulated, and victimized. To us, anger is a weapon that others can use against us.

Our inability to cope with anger in a constructive way makes chemical use attractive for relief of the distress.

The Anger Cycle

Expressing our anger improperly creates harmful consequences. As figure 4 shows, we fall into a cycle of responses that keeps us stuck.

Figure 4: Unjust Treatment or Loss of Control

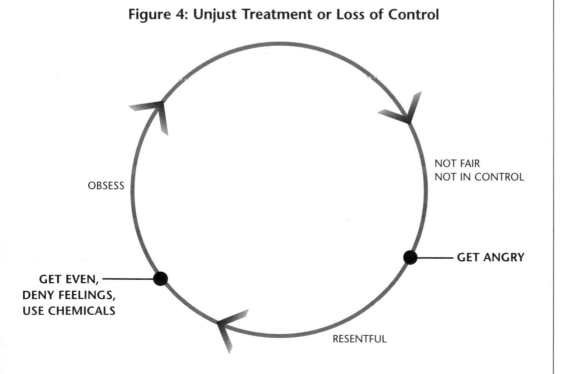

OBSESS

NOT FAIR
NOT IN CONTROL

GET EVEN,
DENY FEELINGS,
USE CHEMICALS

GET ANGRY

RESENTFUL

The anger cycle begins when we perceive that we are being treated unjustly or when we experience a lack of control. We need to identify our anger and resolve it. *If we are skilled at handling our emotions, we can stop the process.* Left unchecked, our anger becomes resentment. As our resentments build, we try to deal with the discomfort in one of three ways:

1. We deny that the anger still affects us. We stuff it into our "emotional backpack" and believe that we have dealt with it. As we continue to stuff emotions into our "backpack," we reach the breaking point, and our anger spills out onto others. We can also turn that anger inward. Inward-directed anger can result in depression.

2. We attempt to "get even." We perceive that we can even things up or right the injustice through some type of retribution, or pay back. We may take an outwardly aggressive stance or quietly get our revenge in a roundabout way. We want to "win."

3. We use chemicals to relieve the discomfort.

The problem with these responses is that they do not resolve the anger. We continue to roll angry thoughts over and over in our minds. Rather than relieve our anger, we increase our sense of injustice and fuel the cycle. Our burning anger creates a heavy spiritual burden.

When we experience anger, it has a direction. In the early stages of recovery, we may direct our anger at one or more of the following:

- The world in general because we can no longer use chemicals. We have to deal with our feelings without the use of drugs and alcohol.

- Family or friends because they intervened to stop our use or they don't understand what we're going through.

- Ourselves for having wasted part of our lives using. Somehow, we should have known better.

- God, or our Higher Power, for making us an addict or alcoholic. "Why me?"

Expressing Anger Appropriately

When we're angry, we need to look closely at the reason. How old is our anger? At whom is our anger directed? Are we angry because someone is not doing something our way? We need to zero in on the specific cause.

1. If our anger results from an irrational belief, that belief needs to be challenged. Chapter 8 gave us ideas for dealing with irrational beliefs.

2. If our anger has a rational basis, we can, if appropriate, let the other person know how we feel. We can calmly use assertive statements such as, "When you behave that way, I feel angry." We don't raise our voices or assume a threatening posture. We want to avoid a verbal contest of who can shout the loudest.

3. If the anger is about a current situation, we can resolve the issue or get out of the situation.

4. We can talk about our feelings with other people. Venting about anger dissipates some of its strength.

5. Forgiving others is a powerful tool for freeing ourselves of resentments.

6. Sometimes there may be no way to right the injustice. It's out of our control. Then we must exercise acceptance. It's called letting go: the understanding that we're powerless to change the situation. The worst thing we can do is worry about some past event that we can't change.

[see example 33] 👉

Tony had learned skills associated with Rational Emotive Behavior Therapy to work through anger issues. He found he did not have to react to others in an angry fashion. He also remembered that it took a lot of practice before he could quickly handle these situations.

PERSONAL STORIES

Example 33. An angry customer came into Tony's store and complained about a product she had purchased there. Her tirade got his own anger rising. Tony quickly identified his reaction and saw that his beliefs—that no one should ever criticize him, that he must never be wrong— caused his anger. He challenged his beliefs and accepted the customer's complaint as valid. He was able to refrain from an angry response and resolve the problem without emotional distress.

 EXERCISE 9a

What are your three most powerful resentments? To whom are they directed?

1. Resentment: _____
   To Whom: _____

2. Resentment: _____
   To Whom: _____

3. Resentment: _____
   To Whom: _____

 EXERCISE 9b

Pick one of the resentments you listed in exercise 9a. Use the REBT process described in chapter 8 to identify and to challenge your belief.

Remember:

Unresolved Anger

↓

Resentments

↓

Relapse to Chemical Use

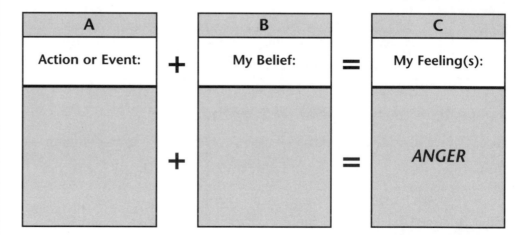

A		B		C
Action or Event:	**+**	**My Belief:**	**=**	**My Feeling(s):**
	+		**=**	*ANGER*

Was your belief an example of not being in control? If so, how can you resolve your anger? How can you challenge your irrational belief?

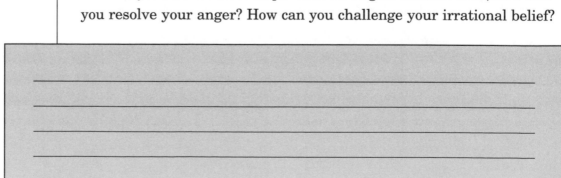

Fear and Worry

Fear is a normal emotion. Overcoming fears moves us forward and creates joy. Fear left unchecked, however, can be a major block to our recovery.

Fear is common in early sobriety. Most of us are apprehensive about new situations. Some of us have never functioned in society as a sober individual. The thought of what's ahead can be overwhelming.

We've learned that the best way to be safe and free from fear is to try to control everything. The problem comes when we have to admit that we have very little control. For alcoholics and addicts, lack of control does not feel safe. It spawns all manner of concerns and fears.

Some of us will find it difficult to identify our fear and will turn it into anger. Some of us will find ourselves overwhelmed by fear and feel out of control and panicked. At times we will feel confident, sometimes too much so. Overconfidence and cockiness are dangerous in sobriety. These attitudes minimize the severity of our addiction or the amount of effort needed to work through our fears. We must always give addiction its due respect.

For many of us, fear is a way of life, a constant companion. The fears we suppressed with chemicals are still there when we get sober. In sobriety, our fears may even be magnified. Some of us have resisted looking at these feelings for years. At times, these excessive fears can paralyze us.

Afraid to Change; Afraid to Stay the Same

Alcoholics and addicts in early sobriety have many fears in common.

- *Living a life without chemicals.* A life without chemicals is a frightening thought. We ask ourselves: How we will cope? What will we do when we feel overwhelmed by emotions? Is our social life centered around using? What excitement could a life without chemicals hold?

  We see that we have to make changes in our friends and lifestyle, but we don't have to make all the changes today. We learn and make progress. We have patience and faith in the recovery process.

- *Changing or losing relationships.* Perhaps all our friends are alcoholics, addicts, or abusers. Now these people threaten our sobriety. If our spouse or partner is addicted and we've decided not to use, how will our abstinence affect that relationship?

Some of our friends are not addicts, but they may occasionally use drugs or alcohol. If we ask them not to use around us, will they still want our company? What will we be like sober?

Becoming sober changes how we interact with others. Sometimes the relationships we built while using lose their charm in recovery. It's possible that we will lose some relationships. Sobriety also allows us to have satisfying and happy relationships. We'll be capable of repairing problems in valuable relationships. New friends await us in the recovery community.

- *Facing the future.* It's scary to start a whole new way of life. How will we figure out the rules? Will they work for us? Will we be able to stay straight?

Sometimes we have to make radical changes in our lives over time. When we experience fear, we may be projecting about the future or living in the past. We may wonder if it's even worth trying to sober up. Worrying about the future blocks us from living in the present. We need to live *one day at a time.* Fear shows a lack of faith in both ourselves and the power of a recovery program involving other sober people.

- *Facing the past.* No amount of worry or anguish will change the past. It's gone. The past will only have as much power as we choose to give it. We get caught up in wondering if only we would've done this, then things would be different. Maybe we wouldn't be an alcoholic or an addict. How can we make up for past mistakes?

This type of worry leads to feelings of anxiety. We can't change the past. It's difficult to deal with the mistakes and trauma of our past. We wouldn't do those things sober. We fear having to face people we harmed through our alcohol and other drug use. We may have past legal or financial issues that now must be confronted.

The past may also hold memories of abuse, abandonment, hopelessness, or shame. We realize that now we must face these issues. We can be overwhelmed by the magnitude of these emotions.

- *Facing others.* What will other people think? How can we face anyone? What will they say when they find out?

We had our own prejudice against drunks and druggies. Now we wonder if others will shun us when they find out. We find ourselves embarrassed to call or see old friends. We're ashamed of our addiction.

Many of us will try to remain in recovery without making the necessary lifestyle changes. We believe that if we choose not to make the tough changes we will somehow get by—so long as we stay abstinent. This approach is rarely successful. If we're afraid and can't face recovery alone, we need to ask for help.

We can waste a lot of energy dealing with fear. The next time we're caught up in fear and worry, we can think about the following statistics:

- Forty percent of our fears never happen.
- Thirty percent of our fears are about the past—things that can't be changed.
- Twelve percent of our fears are based on others' criticisms, most of which are untrue.
- Ten percent of our fears are about health matters that only get worse with worry.
- Eight percent of our fears are legitimate.

Think about it. For many of us, 92 percent of our worries are unproductive. We have the choice of devoting time to worrying or to enjoying life. Which will we choose?

We can manage our fear if we take it slowly, piece by piece. Think of fear as **_Face Everything And Recover_**. Facing the fear is the first part. With the help of our friends in recovery, we can do together what we can't do alone. Others have been through this before. We can let them guide us.

Methods of Coping with Fear

The following list contains things we can do to manage our fear.

- *Accept that fear is normal.* We can choose to be uncomfortable just for today rather than use chemicals.
- *Live one day at a time.* Worrying about the future or trying to change the past stops us from living in the present.
- *Take problems one at a time.* We don't have to resolve problems all at once. We can choose a small problem and work through it with the help of others. Taking problems one at a time reduces the overwhelming nature of our fear.

- *Rely on a Higher Power.* Some of us have a specific concept of a Higher Power (see chapter 11). Fear keeps us stuck. Faith moves us forward. A Higher Power, trust, faith, and recovering friends can get us through life's challenges.

- *Believe.* We need to believe in ourselves and in our recovery.

- *Avoid the extremes.* We shouldn't be too cocky or too afraid. A little apprehension is healthy.

- *Work a strong recovery program.* We need to contact recovering friends, attend recovery groups, and help others.

- *Engage in constructive daily activities.* Idle time gives us the opportunity to worry about things we can't change.

- *Use the "dump-it" button.* If we can't change something right now, we press the dump-it button and forget about it. This method is not scientific, but it is effective!

When you admit to your fears, you start the process of resolution. What are your three biggest fears in recovery?

1. _____

_____

_____

2. _____

_____

_____

3. _____

_____

_____

As you learned in chapter 8, your feelings result from your belief system. Pick one of the fears you listed in exercise 9c. Apply the REBT principles from chapter 8.

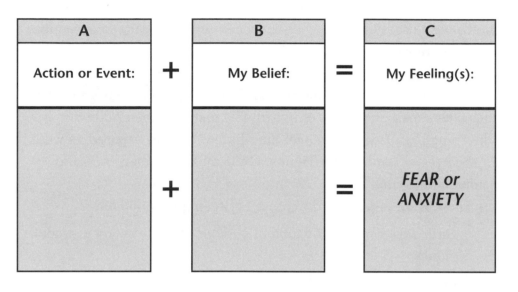

A		B		C
Action or Event:	**+**	**My Belief:**	**=**	**My Feeling(s):**
	+		**=**	*FEAR or ANXIETY*

What did you learn about your beliefs? Is your fear founded in reality? What can you do to resolve or cope with this situation?

Shame versus Guilt

Sometimes we're our harshest critics. We beat ourselves up thinking, "If only I would have done this" or "I should have stopped my chemical use sooner." These mental gymnastics don't solve our problems and leave us feeling like loathsome creatures.

In early recovery, this type of thinking can put us back on the track to chemical use. When we feel like "pond scum," it's easy to rationalize that we are worthless and might as well use to make ourselves feel better for today.

We may say that we understand that this is an illness and not a moral weakness, but most of us still feel dishonorable. Addiction is like being branded, and we feel humiliated. We feel exposed as weak in the eyes of family and friends. Guilt and shame are familiar companions to us.

There is an important difference between guilt and shame:

- Guilt says I made a mistake. I violated the law or my personal values.
- Shame says I *am* a mistake.

👉 *[see examples 34 and 35]*

Shame is counterproductive in recovery. It says that when we make a mistake it's because we're inherently flawed as a person. We are not as good as others or are not worthy of a good life. For some of us, these feelings are not new and preceded our addiction. Using chemicals became a way of dealing with them.

Shame can put us in a dark hole with feelings of despair and self-loathing. Why try to recover or to become who we would like to be when we are naturally flawed? By its nature, shame keeps us from talking to others about how we're feeling—a key factor in recovery. We may believe that exposing our feelings to others will lead to rejection. We've already rejected ourselves. Why wouldn't others also abandon us?

This thinking blocks our recovery and invites us to drink or drug away our pain. We see our addiction as a personal failure, not as a treatable illness.

Example 34. Fran received a speeding ticket. She felt guilty because she was usually quite careful about her driving. She understood that speeding could have injured herself or someone else. She made a commitment to herself to be more careful. Her guilt motivated her to drive more safely in the future.

Example 35. Lois also received a speeding ticket. When she was pulled over, she felt humiliated. She had screwed up again. The ticket proved once more that something was wrong with her. How could she tell anyone about how bad she was? She felt so ashamed she wanted to run and hide. Lois's shame blocks her from dealing with her problems. She thinks she's the mistake.

We can start to change our perception of ourselves by having honest interactions with other recovering people. It's reassuring to find that many of them have the same feelings. When someone we perceive as a "good person" and "having it all together" talks about his or her own personal battle with shame, we realize we're not alone.

When we're open about ourselves and our issues, others react positively to us. This challenges our belief that we are worthless. We learn that these destructive feelings are only *our* perception of who we are, not reality. We see that if we are motivated and willing to risk exploring ourselves, we can make significant changes in our lives.

When we're feeling inadequate, we can take a moment to consider what is really happening. We frequently find that our reaction is inaccurate. We can ask ourselves, "Am I inadequate, or am I just inexperienced?" We may find that we are simply inexperienced in that skill or topic. It is not a matter of personal failure. We can learn to become competent if we so choose. We're reminded that our expectations of ourselves are unrealistically high. Unrealistic expectations lead to feelings of frustration and inadequacy.

List two events that you feel shameful about. Explore these feelings with another recovering person. What is his or her perspective?

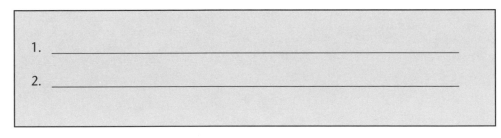

List two situations you feel guilty about.

Remember:

Inadequate

=

Inexperienced

As you learned in chapter 8, your feelings result from your belief system. Pick one of the shameful experiences you listed in exercise 9e. Apply the REBT principles from chapter 8.

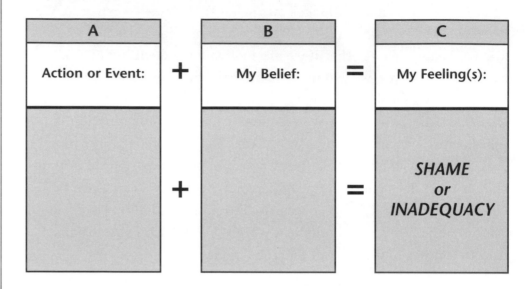

A		B		C
Action or Event:	**+**	**My Belief:**	**=**	**My Feeling(s):**
	+		**=**	*SHAME* *or* *INADEQUACY*

What was your belief system telling you about that event? Is that belief valid?

Ask others in recovery to review this exercise with you.

Grief and the Grieving Process

Grief is the emotional pain we suffer from a loss. When we grieve, we go through several stages—a process. The grieving process is not necessarily predictable—we may jump back and forth from stage to stage.

Any loss, big or small, may trigger the grieving process. We might grieve the loss of a person, place, or relationship. We may grieve a consequence of our chemical use or "what might have been."

The degree of our sense of loss depends on the intensity of our attachment to who or what was lost or on the depth of our loss. What others believe about our loss is unimportant. The loss of a loved pet may feel more devastating than the loss of an abusive husband. What is important is that we recognize our loss and begin to resolve it.

Grieving is common in early recovery. We may have suppressed our grief over the loss of a child, spouse, partner, parent, or other relationship by using drugs or alcohol. We have only postponed the inevitability of having to deal with the resulting grief. Grief is a process that needs to be faced and completed. To do less is to be continually caught in the cycle.

Grieving can take place in stages.

1. *Denial.* We deny or ignore the reality of what's happened. We refuse to face the facts. We rationalize or make excuses to avoid feeling hurt.

2. *Anger.* We're angry that something we value has been taken away. It does not seem fair. We don't feel in control. Our anger is sometimes directed at the person we lost. "How could you do this to me?"

3. *Bargaining.* We look for some way to regain what we've lost. We pray for our loss to be reinstated in some way. We may blame ourselves and promise to change.

4. *Depression.* We come to realize that the person, place, or thing is truly gone.

5. *Acceptance.* We come to accept the loss as reality and move on.

Even when we accept loss, our feelings do not disappear. When we reflect on the person, place, or thing, we feel sadness. Acceptance does not mean that we've eliminated our feelings and are no longer emotionally involved. We simply accept the reality of our loss and how it affects our lives. We can still feel the sadness.

PERSONAL STORIES

Example 36. When Kay's mother passed away, Kay was surprised by her intense feelings of anger toward her mother. How could she feel this way when her mother had just died? She felt guilty, like a bad daughter. A friend explained that when her mother died, Kay lost not only her mother, but also her confidant, a home she could always return to if she had problems in life, unconditional love, and safety. These were "taken away" with her mother's death. Kay's fear had turned to anger at her mother. This was not an uncommon reaction.

Not resolving grief can result in our becoming stuck at some stage of the process. We may jump back to an earlier stage or skip back and forth. We can carry anger and resentment, a sense of abandonment, or a feeling of being incomplete for years. Time alone does not heal all wounds. Time and *attention* will lessen the severity and impact of our feelings. We put our loss in perspective and move on with our lives.

In some cases, we experience guilt in the grieving process. It's normal to sometimes direct our anger at the very person we've lost. We feel guilty about doing this and try to deny our feelings: "A good person wouldn't feel this way."

👉 *[see example 36]*

One grief most of us experience is the loss of our chemicals. When we are confronted with our alcohol or other drug problems, we *deny* that it's true. When we finally realize the truth, we become *angry*. The thought of losing our way of dealing with the world can leave us fearful. We try to *bargain*. Perhaps we can use just once in a while or use a different chemical? When the reality of not being able to control our use hits home, we become *depressed*. As we begin to understand our addiction, we learn to *accept* it and to live with it.

EXERCISE 9g

1. List some significant losses in your life._____

_____

_____

2. Which has been the most painful? _____

3. What stage of the grieving process are you in?_____

   How does it affect your life today? _____

   _____

   _____

4. What is one method you could use to help in accepting this loss? (Ask others in recovery for help in developing a method of resolution.)

   _____

   _____

5. Discuss these feelings with recovering friends to gain more insight.

Daily Journaling

Some of us may want to do "graduate" work on our emotions. The best way to explore our emotions and behavior is through daily journaling. If we keep a daily journal of how we're feeling, we gain skill in identifying our emotions. We begin to recognize behaviors we can change. We also may find distinct patterns in our feelings.

[see example 37] ☞

 9h

Journaling works best when done on a daily basis. Get a notebook or a journal. Try to choose the most significant incident of each day. What event seemed most important or triggered the greatest emotional response within you? Try to be *very* specific about how you were feeling and what happened. You may want to use the feelings list in chapter 8.

You can try using the following format each day:

Example 37. Frank began to keep a daily journal. As he reviewed it, he found that 80 percent of his daily problems related to his wanting to be in control of everyone and everything. He was able to zero in on a major issue.

---

1. *Issue:* (What happened?)

2. *Emotions:* (What emotions or feelings did this event trigger within me?)

3. *What does this tell me about myself?* (How does my reaction fit with what I believe?)

4. *How can I be different?* (How can I change? How can I start to react in a healthier manner?)

Example:

1. *Issue:*

   A friend asked me to do something I didn't think was right. I said yes and went along with it even though I was uncomfortable.

2. *Emotions:*

   Anger, Fear.

3. *What does this tell me about myself?*

   It points out that I'm still trapped in my need to get approval from others. I get angry with myself when I don't stand up for what I believe. I fear what others will think if I speak up. I fear the conflict that may result if I disagree. This focuses on my belief that if I speak up everything will fall apart, that conflict is not okay, that I will sacrifice my personal beliefs for approval.

4. *How can I be different?*

   I can be more responsive to my true feelings and confront them immediately rather than stuff them. This requires me to be more honest and to risk that someone will disapprove. I can believe that feeling better about myself takes priority over what someone else thinks.

We can look through our journals occasionally to see patterns in our behavior. As we start to analyze and identify ways to change, we start to make progress. It takes time and work to initiate changes in our thinking and behaviors. We shouldn't fall prey to impatience, but keep going!

Remember:

- Learning to talk about feelings is a critical part of recovery.
- When dealing with troublesome emotions, we need to use coping skills, communicate with others, and make changes.
- Four emotions seem to persist in early recovery: anger, fear, shame, and grief. We may have used drugs and alcohol to suppress these emotions.
- Anger can be expressed in a positive way.
- Unresolved anger, or resentment, keeps us stuck and miserable in the anger cycle.
- We need to examine the reason for our anger and work to resolve it.
- Realizing we can't control everything can make us fearful. We can tackle fears piece by piece.
- Guilt says I made a mistake; shame says I am a mistake.
- Honesty with ourselves and others helps us improve our perception of ourselves.
- Grief is the emotional pain we suffer from a loss. The five stages of grief are denial, anger, bargaining, depression, and acceptance.
- We may grieve the loss of our chemicals.
- Daily journaling helps us work through our emotions.

Chapter 10
Compulsive Behavior And Isolation

I must NEVER be uncomfortable emotionally OR physically! I must NEVER be uncomfortable EMOTIONALLY! I must NEVER be uncomfortable EVER! I must NEVER be uncomfortable PHYSICALLY! I must NEVER EVER be...

he previous chapter looked at the importance of dealing with our emotions to stay sober. Anger, fear, shame, and grief can sidetrack our recovery. We can also get sidetracked by behaving compulsively and by isolating ourselves.

Compulsive behaviors and isolation provide an escape from our emotions that can bring us down quickly. Exploring ourselves can be a painful process. Some of us choose not to deal with self-discovery. It's easier to focus on someone or something else than to risk changing ourselves or feeling our feelings. This addictive thinking brings us back to the addict and alcoholic's credo: "I should never be uncomfortable, physically or emotionally. If I am, I must end it with all due haste."

Now that we've given up chemicals to change our mood, we may start to look for substitutes. We look to other activities to get our high. If some is good, more is better, and excess is best. We easily substitute compulsive behavior for getting high when we feel bad.

What's Wrong with Compulsive Behavior?

When we turn to compulsive behaviors, we're not changing our addictive behavior, only our method of coping.

Compulsive behaviors seem acceptable because they

- enable us to avoid looking at our own problems or our addiction
- make us feel good in the short term
- give us the illusion that we are doing okay because we're not getting high on chemicals

Compulsive behaviors can lead us back to chemical use because they

- don't give us as good a feeling as using chemicals did. We switch back to chemicals for a better high.
- can be self-destructive in their own right. We create new problems in our lives. We may go back to chemical use for relief from our new problems.
- convince us we don't need to spend much time on our recovery. We focus on the compulsive behavior and believe our recovery is going well. We believe that minimal efforts to stay sober are enough. Denying the severity of our addiction brings us back to chemical use.

Some Common Reasons for Compulsive Behavior

We may turn to compulsive behaviors for several reasons.

- It's easy to see ourselves as having fallen behind our peers. We think we need to make up for time lost to our addiction.
- We seek approval.
- We want to avoid looking at the real issues.

☞ [see example 38]

Example 38. After six weeks of sobriety, Michael wanted to get on with his life. He was thirty-two years old and still working menial jobs. Michael said that he needed career training. Both his brother and sister were doctors. Michael started to focus on getting into school and began working two part-time jobs to help pay for everything. Soon he was back to alcohol and drug use.

Nothing was wrong with Michael's plan except the timing. He needed to be stable in recovery first. It's easy to lose sight of what's important and become impatient when we believe we need to make up for lost time. We have a need to prove to ourselves and others that we're okay. This kind of thinking helps us rationalize compulsive behavior, such as working long hours or taking on two jobs. We need to focus on recovery. Without that, our other desires become unattainable. We need to *slow down!*

What Are Some Common Compulsive Behaviors?

There are several types of compulsive behavior.

Eating

Many of us find that our food intake changes in recovery. Some of us will crave chocolate and other sweets. Stopping our chemical use can help us identify ongoing eating disorders such as bulimia or anorexia. We can't be afraid to ask for help. Food disorders can be life threatening.

Cleanliness

Another way to ease anxieties is to clean to perfection. When we feel a lot of anxiety or like we're losing control, we strive for order by being compulsive about our surroundings. A clean and clutter-free environment is healthy in many respects, but overdoing it may mean we're avoiding issues of control or fear.

Tobacco Use

We either start smoking or increase the number of cigarettes we smoke. Some of us switch to smokeless tobacco in an attempt to control our cigarette use but end up becoming addicted to smokeless tobacco.

Gambling

Gambling offers action, escape, and great emotional highs and lows. Casino gambling brings the additional excitement of glamour, lights and sounds, and, of course, drugs and alcohol.

Gambling can be addictive. Many of the same principles of chemical addiction apply to gambling, and the consequences to health and family can be just as devastating. Financial ruin for the compulsive gambler is almost always inevitable.

Spending

The act of shopping and buying is a high to some. If we shop compulsively, we can end up with thousands of dollars of credit-card debt in no time at all. Material things can make us feel good for a while, but overspending creates financial problems and stress, leading us back to chemical use.

Using Computers and the Internet

As computers and the Internet become common in most homes, addicted people find a ready-made site for compulsive activities. It's easy to become absorbed in an exciting computer game and spend hours playing.

The Internet offers interactions with others in a safe environment. No one knows us on the Internet, and we can get attention without risking emotional intimacy. We can create fantasy lives. We find ourselves forsaking normal activities and relationships to spend time online. We withdraw from the support system we need to maintain our recovery.

Forming Relationships/Focusing on Sex

Relationships and sex can be a great diversion from having to focus on our own issues. We may view a new relationship as a quick fix to a bad relationship. These new relationships feel warm and fuzzy—much better than the harsh reality of dealing with the consequences of our addiction. We rationalize our behavior by believing that this person is just what we needed: "Our Higher Power put this person in our lives."

Some of us may build up credit-card debt by calling sex-oriented phone lines frequently. We may be too ashamed to get help for this compulsion. It seems "dirty" to us. Not being honest just prolongs the agony and increases the severity of our consequences.

Overworking

Overwork, or "workaholism," gets us much needed approval. It can be another way of trying to make up for lost time. It easily takes us away from practicing a program of recovery and fuels the idea that perhaps sobriety isn't all that difficult.

Exercising

We can exercise to feel better about ourselves, but our impatience can drive us to make extreme changes in body image quickly. It's a behavior that can result in approval from others, further reinforcing the compulsion. It may also be a sign of an eating disorder. We need to exercise in moderation.

Isolation and Withdrawal

Another way to avoid dealing with our feelings is to isolate ourselves. When we're alone, we have more control in our lives. We can avoid dealing with bills, relationships, responsibilities, and our own addiction. We don't have to interact with other people. When we're alone, we can construct our own reality and no one will challenge our thinking. This can include deciding to use chemicals again.

Some will ask, "Isn't it good to withdraw once in a while?" We need to distinguish between isolation and solitude. Solitude is recognizing the need to take time for ourselves. We read a book, take a walk in the woods, or stay in for the evening to watch a movie on TV. It's a time to wind down, center ourselves, and focus on our priorities. "Downtime" is necessary in this fast-paced world.

What makes isolation different is the intent. We're not relaxing or centering ourselves, we're escaping. We're looking for ways to avoid dealing with the responsibilities in our lives. It just all seems so frightening.

We withdraw to a place where we believe we feel safe. There is no healing here, only constant thinking about problems. When we do this, we isolate ourselves from our support system. We stay stuck or make our problems worse because we're not dealing with them. Isolation puts us one step closer to a return to chemical use.

It's easy for us to rationalize our attempts at isolation as normal. We need to be discerning. We should let others know about our solitary activities and see what they think. They may have a better perspective.

Example 39. Steve went on a spending spree because he felt unwanted and worthless. It created severe financial problems for him, and he was forced to move from a safe, sober living situation to a low-rent apartment in a neighborhood where there was lots of drug use. Steve soon found himself back drinking and drugging.

Example 40. Jennifer wanted to regain the high-class lifestyle that she had attained several years before hitting bottom. Living in luxury would prove to others that she was okay. Jennifer needed to work long hours to earn the money she needed. It felt good to receive praise for her efforts and to make a good living. However, working long hours meant that she could no longer attend recovery meetings or meet with sober friends. She gradually forgot that she was dealing with a terminal illness. The HALT symptoms—Hungry, Angry, Lonely, Tired—quickly became part of her life. She finally chose chemical use as a solution for her emotional stress.

Undermining Our Foundation

If we get sidetracked from our program of personal growth through compulsive behavior and isolation, we slide back down the recovery slope. We end up in high-risk situations, having using urges, and destabilizing our recovery lifestyle. Compulsive behaviors and isolation can sabotage the basic foundations of the recovery program described in chapter 5.

Stable Living Situation

☞ *[see example 39]*

Steve's new neighborhood was an extremely dangerous living situation for him. Compulsive behavior directly affected the stability of his recovery from drug use.

Stable Recovery Support System

☞ *[see example 40]*

Jennifer found that recovery needs to be a priority. Everything else happens because of it. Isolation and "workaholism" couldn't keep her sober. She needed the help of her recovery support system.

Stable Job or Daily Activities

[see example 41] ☞

Rick found that it does not take long for an alcoholic or addict to replace one addiction with another. In early recovery, we need structure and accountability. We need to put discipline into our self-centered lifestyle and attitudes.

Stable Relationships

[see example 42]

Lynn had quickly eroded her relationship with her husband and children. They saw her as displaying all the dishonesty and self-centeredness that she had while using—a return to a "dry drunk." In her search for feeling good without alcohol, Lynn had sacrificed her family support. With the emotional turmoil and self-loathing she had created, a return to chemical use was only a matter of time.

✦✦✦

As we can see, compulsive behaviors and isolation can break down the foundation of our recovery. They can cloud our thinking and allow us to be in high-risk situations or to look for relief in self-defeating ways. We may not be aware that we have reverted to compulsive behaviors. We sometimes see them as positive solutions to daily problems. We need to be cautious, to be honest about our "agenda," and to listen to the recommendations of others in recovery.

EXERCISE 10a

Are there compulsive behaviors that you've already had to deal with? Do you recognize behaviors you could be vulnerable to in the future?

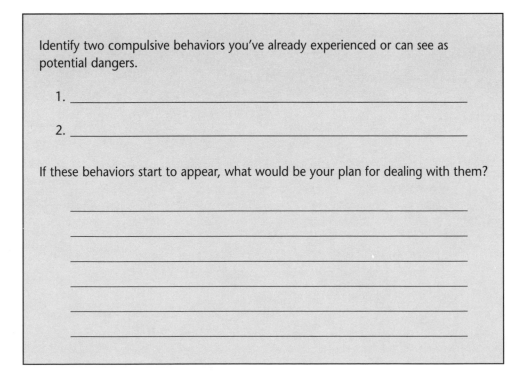

Identify two compulsive behaviors you've already experienced or can see as potential dangers.

1. _____

2. _____

If these behaviors start to appear, what would be your plan for dealing with them?

_____
_____
_____
_____
_____
_____

PERSONAL STORIES

Example 41. Rick felt bored in recovery. He had too much time on his hands now that he wasn't using cocaine. He missed the excitement of the "drug world." Rick decided that he didn't have to change his laid-back lifestyle or friends. He went with an old friend to a casino. The excitement and action gave Rick a psychological high, plus there was access to drugs and alcohol. He found he could "drink free" while he was gambling. Soon Rick was going to the casino every day and drinking heavily.

Example 42. Lynn, a recovering alcoholic, had always gotten good feelings by associating with men. Her girlfriends called her a "love junkie." Unhappy in her marriage, Lynn started to see a male friend. Lynn's husband found out about her affair and locked her out of the house. Her grown children were angry at her behavior and would not talk to her. Suddenly everything seemed to be crashing in on her. Lynn began drinking again to cope with her distress.

Remember:

- Recovery is not the first priority; it's the only priority. We must be patient.
- Compulsive behaviors occur quickly and easily. They're a method of avoiding reality.
- Exploring our emotions and taking responsibility for our behavior is part of recovery.
- We need to check our thinking and activities with others. We can easily rationalize unhealthy behaviors.
- We shouldn't assume that we will know what's best for us.
- There will be a natural tendency to withdraw when encountering intense feelings. We need to fight this tendency.
- Feeling bad is a part of life, and we need to deal with it.
- Solitude and isolation are different. We should know the difference and not delude ourselves that isolation is okay.

Chapter 11
SPIRITUALITY AND RECOVERY

As we progress in early sobriety, we focus on the practical side of recovery—abstaining, avoiding high-risk situations, stabilizing our lifestyle, and learning coping skills. Along with building our practical skills, we must find spirituality.

Developing a spiritual nature is critical because our level of spirituality greatly impacts how we feel about ourselves and others. But many of us struggle with the spiritual aspect of recovery. This is especially true if we've had difficult experiences with religion in the past.

Well, I've READ all these books, and I KNOW I'm an ADDICT, so I just KNOW I'll stay SOBER!

We need to set aside any prejudice against religion we might have. We must also set aside our concepts of what "God" should be. We don't have time to cynically scrutinize religious beliefs or theories of the universe. These are useless exercises for us. Keeping an open mind is essential.

The concept of spirituality is a very personal one. Spirituality is the quality of our relationship with ourselves, our Higher Power, the world, and all the people in it. It encompasses our values, our priorities, the way we interact with others, and our concept of a Higher Power. We can be spiritual without being religious and vice versa.

Many of us tried to "play God" during our using days. We believed we had the ultimate plan for ourselves and others. We alone were endowed with the ability to "be right." We tried to make others conform to our own ideas of how the world should be. Our quest for power and control crushed any spiritual nature we had.

When we searched for happiness, we found a void, or spiritual emptiness, in our lives. We tried to fill that void with alcohol or other drugs, money, relationships, material things, or compulsive behaviors of one type or another. We found these external answers didn't resolve our internal needs. We had to search for another solution.

When we're challenged by severe urges to drink or drug, our whole being, mentally and physically, wants to return to our addiction. We need to remember that *the knowledge that we're addicted to alcohol or other drugs will not keep us sober.* If we remain as spiritually bankrupt as we were in our using days, we will return to our old behaviors and, ultimately, chemical use.

What Is a Spiritual Awakening?

A spiritual awakening can be described as a change in attitude, behavior, and thinking. An awakening does not need to be a monumental event. It can be as simple as being able to feel overwhelmed with joy when watching a sunset.

A spiritual awakening comes about naturally as a result of working a recovery program and believing that we need to grasp the concept of a power greater than ourselves. Self-centered behavior, anger, and resentments are removed. We develop an attitude of understanding and of being helpful to others. We find we have a place in this world where we're happy and fulfilled without alcohol and other drugs and without resorting to compulsive behaviors.

These are changes that we, as individuals, couldn't achieve by will-power alone. These changes are truly miracles.

[see example 43]

Is Carmen a miracle? It certainly seemed that way. How could she finally change when the answer had escaped her for so long? She needed help from a power greater than herself to accomplish what she could not do alone. If we're looking for recovery, we must develop a spiritual sense that brings us peace and serenity.

Relying on a Higher Power

When we seek a Higher Power, be it a supreme being or other recovering friends, we have the faith and courage to carry on. We are whole without chemicals. Our spiritual nature is the insurance we draw on to resist the urges to return to old behavior and chemical use.

Some of us resist the idea of a Higher Power because we associate it with old ideas about religious beliefs—perhaps an authoritarian God that we've rejected. We're talking about a broader kind of Higher Power here.

A Higher Power can be defined in many ways. Some people may call their Higher Power *God*. For others it is the inherent greatness of nature and the universe. For some of us it may be a group of recovery friends whose collective wisdom is greater than our own. Some call their Higher Power *G.O.D.* for "Group Of Drunks" or "Good Orderly Direction."

A belief in God or religion is not necessary. What is necessary is grasping the idea that we can't achieve sobriety alone.

Some of us may panic because we don't know who God is or don't have any concept of a Higher Power. But we can relax. A person with many years of recovery once said, "You don't have to know who God is; all you have to know is you ain't God." It's really that simple. We have to stop playing God, thinking we should know all the answers and be completely self-sufficient. We can ask for help.

Whatever we believe, we must embrace the notion that we need help in making the changes in our lives that recovery demands. No matter what the religious orientation of those of us who seek recovery—atheist, agnostic, Christian, Jew, Muslim, or something else—we can't do it alone. When we know we can't do it alone, a leap of faith seems easier to make.

PERSONAL STORIES

Example 43. After using alcohol and other drugs for years, Carmen had crossed the line into addiction. She tried to quit by herself numerous times with no success. Carmen prayed for an answer. Eventually, she found help for her addiction—a chemical dependency treatment program. Carmen discovered that with guidance and support, she no longer had to use chemicals. Her personality changed. Rather than blame and resent others, she started being happy and feeling gratitude. She treated others with kindness and respect. Her friends said, "She's changed. What a miracle!"

How Do I Become More Spiritual?

There are no easy rules for finding spirituality. It's a journey. The following are aspects of spirituality we need to incorporate into our program of recovery.

- Faith
- Surrender, or "letting go"
- Acceptance
- Humility
- Gratitude
- Meditation and prayer

Faith

Believing that everything works out just the way it is supposed to is a difficult concept to grasp. If we attempt our journey without faith, we put forth only part of the energy needed to succeed.

Faith and trust are usually won by experience and commitment. By examining the experiences of others who have faced the same challenges, we learn that our needs will be met but that we must do the work. *We're responsible for the effort not the outcome.* Faith alone will not solve our problems. Faith and the *willingness to take action* will start us on our way to spiritual development.

Having faith, which also means having trust, won't necessarily take our fears away: Meeting the challenges in life means facing our fears. We need faith to give us strength and courage. Faith gives us the ability to move on in spite of our fears.

Sometimes we'll need the help of others to accomplish what needs to be done. When we're unsure of our course of action, we can use prayer or the wisdom of others for guidance. We use a Higher Power to accomplish what we can't do alone.

Faith means believing that everything will happen in its own time. Our impatience with not getting what we want sets us up for anger and resentments.

[see example 44]

Example 44. Scott had lost most of his material possessions before he finally got sober. After six months of sobriety, he was still without a car or a nice apartment. Scott's recovery sponsor told him to continue working hard at recovery and that he would get what he needed when he was ready for it. Scott was not entirely satisfied with that answer, but he tried to have faith that what he heard was true. After three years of recovery, Scott looked back and saw that he had received more than he had ever envisioned.

Life has its own timetable. Our problem is that it's not *our* time-table. Our quest for the quick fix and immediate gratification denies the fact that life is difficult and success and spiritual growth are won on a daily basis. Impatience forces us to rush for external solutions to our internal problems. Problems of arrogance, grief, anger, selfishness, and fear take time to resolve. We need faith to keep us on a steady course of growth.

Surrender, or "Letting Go"

Surrendering, or conceding that we're not in control, is the next step in beginning a spiritual journey. When we let go, we make space for our Higher Power.

At first we may see surrendering as failing or begrudgingly giving up. Letting go is not about failure; it's about giving up trying to change things that are beyond our influence. It's not weakness; it's changing the things we can. We stop trying to force the square peg into the round hole.

This concept of letting go is foreign to many of us. We're used to trying to be in control, and when we're not, we try to control that much harder. We find that we can't control our chemical use; more-over, we have little control over other people, places, and things.

Letting go means keeping our expectations simple. Serenity usually depends on our expectations. If we set our expectations too high or on the unachievable, we're constantly frustrated and upset. Once we step aside, we feel a new sense of freedom and relief. It takes enormous energy to try to control everything. When we let go of control, we free up that energy and use it for positives in our lives.

We need to develop a manner of living that focuses on what can be changed in *our* lives. We learn to let go of those things we can't change. This means giving up control and our efforts to have the world *our* way. We replace the struggle to keep control with the beliefs that

- we're not in control and can't play God
- we can't resolve our addiction and self-centeredness alone

Acceptance

Letting go also means accepting the world as it is. Accepting ourselves and others is crucial in the development of our spirituality. We're searching for peace and serenity. In the past we became angry because other people were not doing things *our way*. We believed that we knew how people should behave—*our way*. Now we accept that we have little control over others.

We accept life on life's terms. Trying to control other people and situations is destructive when we're trying to build a spiritual program. We need to appreciate that others may have differing views. Everyone has their own values and behaviors based on their life experiences. These experiences may differ drastically from our own. What seems right for us may not be right for them.

Imagine a Catholic priest and an Orthodox Jewish rabbi discussing religion. Could either convince the other that his life's commitment is wrong and that he should change religions? Not likely. We can't project our beliefs on others. When we do, we may be saying that all the experiences that formed their values and attitudes are wrong or irrelevant. Needless to say, if we try to invalidate someone's life experiences, we meet with much resistance, anger, and resentment.

We must accept others just as they are—people who make mistakes but who are valuable and lovable nonetheless. As we become able to accept others and to not be judgmental, we're able to apply this principle to ourselves as well.

We can only accept ourselves when we're honest about who we are. When we accept our addiction and using behavior, we begin the path to self-acceptance. We no longer have to project an image of who we think we *should* be. We become content with who we really are.

Acknowledging the truth about ourselves and our chemical use and accepting our powerlessness over chemicals takes away the shame of our past behavior. We did things we regret, and we become willing to take responsibility for them. It's too easy to condemn ourselves and our behavior. We sustain our recovery by being gentle with ourselves, by nurturing our acceptance of ourselves, and by living life on life's terms.

Humility

Humility is a concept that many of us struggle with. We confuse humility with humiliation. We mistakenly think of humility as being held up to others as less than adequate or flawed. We picture being ashamed or not being given our proper place.

Being humble doesn't mean thinking less of ourselves; it means thinking of ourselves less often. It is seeing ourselves as we really are, not as we'd like ourselves to be. It is a freedom from false pride and arrogance.

We understand the relationship between ourselves and others. We tolerate our own mistakes as well as those of others. We forgive others. We respect others. We're unselfish in our interactions with others. We face the fact that we're flawed. We focus on our issues rather than on finding fault in others to feel better about ourselves. Humility means we are grateful for what we do have.

Gratitude

Keeping a spiritual attitude involves continually assessing our true state of being. It's easy to slip into "stinking thinking" when starting a recovery program. We find that adjusting to a new lifestyle can spark anger and grief. (Remember that we will grieve the loss of our chemicals.) We can find numerous losses to focus on and create a negative state of mind. This negative thinking leads us back to a desire to use chemicals.

Gratitude is focusing on what we have. Some days we may be grateful only for the fact that we are sober. On other days, we see a multitude of gifts that we have been given. When we have difficulty finding even one positive to be grateful for, we need to contact our recovery support system friends and have them help us. The glass moves from being half empty to half full.

Make a list of what you're grateful for. It may be family, friends, a job, or a roof over your head. Read this list every day as a reminder of what you have to be grateful for.

> 1. _____
> (Hint: Your sobriety today.)
>
> 2. _____
>
> 3. _____
>
> 4. _____

Meditation and Prayer

- Prayer is talking to our Higher Power.
- Meditation is listening to our Higher Power.

Life is frequently fast paced and stressful. We need time to sit back and gain perspective on our daily lives. This can be done through the use of prayer or meditation.

Many of us pray frequently. Some of us have never prayed. If we don't believe in prayer, we need to act as if we do. We can try praying and see what happens. Our prayers do not have to be complex.

Sometimes using the Serenity Prayer is as much as we can do: *God grant me the serenity to accept the things I cannot change, the courage to change the things I can, and the wisdom to know the difference.* We are praying to be able to accept life on life's terms.

Sometimes we prayed even if we didn't believe in God: "God get me out of this and I promise I'll never drink or drug again." These prayers are self-serving. We try to avoid praying for our own selfish needs. We pray for the courage to change and to confront the situations that frighten us. We pray for others. Even those we don't like. We pray for the resolution of the anger we carry toward some people.

We're not trying to be saints. Instead, we're trying to relieve the fears, grief, and anger that can bring us back to alcohol or other drug use. Our prayers bring a sense of calm and well-being—a sense that

God grant me the serenity to accept the things I cannot change, the courage to change the things I can, and the wisdom to know the difference.

The Serenity Prayer

we're part of a greater whole. It's difficult to drink or drug when we feel spiritually connected to our Higher Power and other people. It's easy to use chemicals when our hearts are full of anger and fear.

Meditation is a wonderful way to get a break from daily stressors. The object is to clear our minds of racing thoughts. We seek to restore a sense of calmness. We learn to listen to our inner selves. Ideas or solutions just come to us. Like most worthwhile things, deep meditation is achieved by practice. Now is a perfect time to start to learn.

 **EXERCISE 11b**

If meditation is new to you, try the following method.

> - Begin by sitting in a comfortable chair, feet flat on the ground.
>
> - Place your arms on the arms of the chair or let them rest comfortably in your lap. Always use a position that's comfortable.
>
> - Center your thoughts on something, such as your breathing.
>
> - Close your eyes and take deep breaths. Focus on feeling the air going in and out of your nose or your diaphragm expanding with each breath.

At first your mind is immediately filled with thoughts of what you should be doing, what needs to be done, and what you should have done two weeks ago. When you find yourself straying to these thoughts, focus on your breathing. Soon, you're able to clear your mind for several minutes, then longer. When obsessive thoughts catch up with you, simply refocus regardless of how many times it takes.

Start with just two minutes and try to work up to fifteen to twenty minutes of meditation. During the day, if you're feeling stressed, you can usually find two minutes to meditate and to slow yourself down. When you don't react out of stress, you make better decisions. You're able to maintain an attitude of gratitude and acceptance.

❖❖❖

Daily prayer and meditation are useful when we encounter strong using urges. Practice pays off when we're able to weather unexpected using thoughts and overwhelming feelings.

It's easy to use chemicals when our hearts are full of anger and fear.

Just for Today:
A Weekly Program of Building Serenity

We can help build our own concept of spirituality by doing just one thing each day of the week.

Day 1. Don't judge anyone today, not even ourselves.

Day 2. Do something nice for someone, but don't let them or anyone else know.

Day 3. Greet everyone we meet with a big smile—grocery clerk, parking attendant, employer.

Day 4. Take fifteen minutes to sit and think about how lucky we are to have what we do have, no matter how simple.

Day 5. Say the Serenity Prayer as frequently as we can.

Day 6. Say a prayer of compassion for someone we *don't* like. We should do so even if we don't believe in prayer. This is for *us* to cleanse the anger and resentments out of our hearts.

Day 7. Call another recovering person and ask how he or she is doing. This gets us to focus outside ourselves.

Remember:

- Some concept of spirituality and a Higher Power is necessary for continued recovery. This does not ask us to believe in God or to go to church.

- We cannot play God. We accept the fact that we don't know everything and must ask for guidance and help from other recovering people. We must lose our self-centeredness—put our arrogance and self-will aside.

- We learn that our impatience is a barrier to our spirituality. The world runs on its own time schedule, not ours.

- We see the idea that faith, acceptance, and gratitude can carry us through even when times are difficult.

- We accept that life is difficult and that we need others to help us on our spiritual journey.

Chapter 12

What do I Tell Others About My Dependency?

Our dependency on alcohol and other drugs is usually not a secret. We may believe we've been careful, but it's hard to hide addiction from those who are close to us. We find that others realized the seriousness of our chemical use long before we did.

Alcohol on our breath, missed appointments, job problems, legal entanglements, unexpected rages, and irresponsible behavior alerted people to our problems. We may have forgotten about some of our outrageous behavior, but those around us haven't.

Most of these people are just glad to see us get the help we deserve. They are genuinely concerned about our well-being. Others, however, harbor great anger and resentments and may confront us about our using behaviors.

It's tempting to try to explain how our addiction is a disease and how we would not have acted that way if we had been sober. We should resist this course of action. What we say at this time will not influence their feelings. The anger is theirs; we can't change how they feel.

We will be confronted about our behavior on many occasions; we can't run from it. This confrontation is one of the consequences we suffer because of our past use. What we can do is to show over time that we've changed.

Avoiding Addiction Evangelism

We're better off keeping a low profile about our dependency. Our self-centeredness may want to focus on our triumph over the "evils of alcohol and drugs." We may feel so virtuous that we become evangelists for recovery.

We become critical of our friends and relatives and suggest they may have a drinking or drugging problem also. We try to tell them how to run their lives. We're beginners in recovery and poor judges of others. We need to focus on ourselves—not others.

We should hold back on our enthusiasm for recovery, partly because of the possibility of a relapse to chemical use. There are many cases of celebrities who have made the "talk-show circuit," discussing their newfound lifestyle, only to end up in the gossip columns several days later as they are readmitted to treatment. Those of us who are not high-profile people can learn from this experience. When others ask us about our recovery, we can tell them, "It's a long journey, and I'm taking it one day at a time."

Our friends and families tire of hastily made amends and bold talk for the future. People want to see changes in our behavior and consistency in our ability to remain off alcohol and other drugs. Most of them have heard our apologies and promises for change before. The best way to handle these situations is with humility and action. We should try to focus on making constructive changes in behavior and attitude for the moment, not on past mistakes or future projections.

What about Family?

Do our families know about our addiction and our attempt at recovery? It's unlikely that we've been able to hide our addiction. But if we have, we may try to avoid being honest with them.

Many times our avoidance is really about our own beliefs of our alcoholism and drug addiction. We may think that we've let our families down, that they will think less of us. We forget that we did not ask for our addiction and are powerless over it. Most family members are happy about and supportive of our recovery. Trying to hide it only allows another secret into our lives. We need to be honest.

Some family members may still be in denial about our addiction. Others may live some distance away and not be familiar with our struggles. They may tell us that we're not really addicted or minimize our consequences. This type of thinking appeals to us, but we should resist buying into it. This inaccurate thinking keeps their world more secure but denies the reality of what's happened to us. It can give us a reason to go back to our chemical use. Our goal is not to please others; it's to progress in recovery.

Parents frequently want to deny our addiction because they're afraid they've done something to cause it or believe it's a shameful thing to have in the family. It is *not* necessary that our families understand our addiction. Some family members will understand in time; others may never understand. The important thing is for us to understand it. Explanations can be simple and focused on what we're doing to stay in recovery.

Family members know how to "push our buttons." Interactions with them can end up being a replay of our drinking and drugging days. We feel ashamed or misunderstood by people who mean much to us. If being around certain family members breeds conflict, we should detach ourselves from them—emotionally and physically, if necessary—for a while. We need time to get our own house in order.

We can't trust our families and friends to keep us sober. Many times we mistakenly believe that friends and family will not let us drink. We find out too late that their denial or fear of saying the wrong thing may stop them from intervening.

Identify the family member you will have the hardest time talking to about your addiction. Write down why the conversation would be difficult.

Family member: _____

Why conversation would be difficult: _____

_____

_____

_____

_____

What about Friends?

Friends may ask a lot of questions if they know we're a recovering alcoholic or addict. It's usually best to be honest about our dependency. These people need to know that we're no longer drinking or drugging. They may attempt to offer us mood-altering chemicals otherwise. While we need to be honest about our addiction, we do not need to share all the details. We have no obligation to volunteer specific information.

We believe our friends have our best interests at heart. Sometimes, though, we find that because they do not understand addiction, they will offer us chemicals.

☞ [see example 45]

It's apparent that, although Jeff's friends know he went through a treatment program, they don't understand addiction. We need to be careful around our friends. We need to tell them in no uncertain terms that we can't use any mood-altering chemicals at all. If we play down the seriousness of our addiction, we're open to temptation.

Example 45. Jeff has just completed a chemical dependency treatment program. His friends all know that he has quit using drugs and alcohol. At the softball game the next week, his teammates offer him a beer. "One beer won't hurt you. Just don't get drunk." "You can still smoke a little weed can't you?" "How long do you have to stay straight? When can you start using again?" "You don't have to go to those meetings do you?"

We may find that some of our friends are simply too dangerous for us to be around. To maintain that friendship, they will have to meet us on our terms—no chemical use. If they choose not to do that, we see that they were not really friends at all—they were "using buddies."

When we change our lifestyle to one of recovery, we will lose some of the people in our lives. The important part to remember is that we can develop relationships with recovering friends who accept us as we are.

EXERCISE 12b

---

1. What friends are most likely to understand your need for abstinence?

   _____

   _____

   _____

2. What friends are most likely to be a danger to your recovery?

   _____

   _____

   _____

What Do We Say to Employers or at a Job Interview?

In our society, if someone "disappears" or is on medical leave for several weeks, some people will assume chemical dependency treatment, especially if the absent person had been behaving erratically.

For many of us, our employers are the ones who intervened and suggested we get professional help for our chemical use. They saw the steady decline in our production or attitude. They saw us after a hard weekend, or they had to find a replacement for us on Mondays because we had the "flu."

If we've been treated for chemical dependency, our employers may ask us to sign a contract stating that if we use chemicals again we will lose our jobs. They may ask us to prove that we are going to AA or receiving ongoing professional help.

We may see these actions as unfair or discriminatory. These requests are neither harsh nor unreasonable. Our employers are concerned about our health and responsible for keeping their work environment safe. We can look at this as further accountability to stay straight. Ultimately, what all of us want is for us to maintain sobriety and to become involved in a stable recovery program.

If we're looking for a job, we'll be faced with the question of whether to mention our dependency on the application or in the job interview. We may be asked to explain gaps in our employment history, frequent job changes, or felony charges.

We must plan in advance how we will answer these questions. We can ask friends in recovery how employers respond to people who are chemically dependent. Many people approach the problem with the philosophy of "if they don't ask, don't tell." We're there to interview for a job, not to discuss personal history.

Insurance forms may ask if we've been to treatment or are addicted. Dishonesty in answering these questions may void our insurance policy. We have to face the consequences of our using.

It's not unusual for us to advance rapidly once our employers are satisfied that we've addressed our chemical issues. A program of recovery changes our attitude and behavior. We're more responsible. We devote time and energy to exploring our character defects and shortcomings. We use Rational-Emotive Therapy to make constructive changes in our lives. We don't blame others for our problems and take responsibility for our own behaviors. Our co-workers may not be as diligent in these areas.

Co-workers

Many of us worry about how our co-workers will react to our addiction. Some may already be aware of our chemical problems while others have no knowledge. If we've been away in an inpatient program, our absence from work will be noticeable.

If we're getting sober by using this workbook at home, through a self-help group, or by attending an outpatient program or counseling sessions, our dependency may be less obvious. We can ask others in recovery about their experiences with co-workers. If we're in doubt about how to approach people, we need to be cautious and to take our time deciding. Only our arrogance convinces us that everyone is wondering about us when in fact few may care.

It's like this: I was a DRUNK, I got SOBER, and now I have a HAPPY life!

Cool!

While we may want to maintain a low profile, we need to be assured that chemical dependency treatment is common in our society today. Sometimes the last thing we need is another secret.

If we know of other recovering people at work, we can get guidance from them about how they've fared. They may know about the level of office gossip on such matters. Some people decide to just say they were on medical leave. Not telling leaves us open to others asking us to participate in drinking or drugging with them and then we need excuses to maintain our confidentiality. We may choose to use rather than to let out our secret.

Some of us may not care what co-workers think. If we are living a program of rigorous honesty, we may stop the gossip by being honest with people about our experiences. At times, this can be the best method. We don't need to supply details or horror stories about our use. The truth is out, and life goes on. There may be short-term discomfort, but it will probably dissipate quickly.

Ultimately, it's difficult to make the perfect decision. We can weigh our options and talk to others for guidance. Regardless of what we decide, we can't let the pressures bring us back to chemical use.

Becoming the Expert

As people see us making dramatic changes in our lives, they may perceive us as people who know all about alcoholism and drug addiction. Some will ask us questions about their own drinking or drugging. Others will want advice on what to do with a friend or family member who they feel has a chemical problem. Because we may be the only recovering person they know, they see us as the expert.

Any information we hear about a person may very well be inaccurate. The person in question can be much worse off than others believe or not have much of a problem at all. We don't need to be giving advice when we're not sure of what's really going on.

We can listen and briefly relate our own story of how we handled our addiction to alcohol and other drugs. We can explain that the illness of addiction is treatable and that the first step is getting a professional assessment. Professionals and self-help recovery groups can be a resource to this person.

One day we may receive a call from a recovery friend or acquaintance. The person is intoxicated and "looking for help." Spending hours on the phone listening to resentments and self-pity or trying to talk that person into stopping his or her use won't help the person and will leave us emotionally drained.

There are numerous examples of someone trying to help another with the result that they both end up using together. If we feel we need to help someone, we *never go to that person alone.* This is not a suggestion, it's a rule. We must *always* take someone more experienced in recovery with us. If the person in need is of the opposite sex, we go with someone who is the same gender as the person in need. Two men should not be intervening with a woman or vice versa.

Remember:

- Our chemical use is more evident to others than we may have thought.
- We need to avoid making promises about keeping sobriety. Others may be sick of promises and want to see changes.
- It is necessary to be honest about our recovery with people close to us. When they know, we close the door to using around them.
- We don't have to supply gruesome details of our use.
- Not everyone will understand or be interested in our addiction. Some may be downright angry. We shouldn't be defensive or try to explain.
- There are consequences for lying about chemical dependency on job applications or insurance forms.
- We should try not to be an "evangelist" or an "expert" on recovery. We focus on our own issues.

Chapter 13
RELATIONSHIPS AND SEX IN RECOVERY

elationships become a major issue in early recovery. For years our most important relationship had been with alcohol and other drugs. We neglected, damaged, or destroyed relationships with our husbands or wives, partners, children, parents, and friends. All of these people have been affected by our chemical use. All of these people will still have issues with us in our recovery.

We may realize that we've always had trouble forming or maintaining relationships, maybe even before we started using chemicals. Our early intimate interactions with others may not have been positive. Some of us learned our relationship skills from parents who fought with, withdrew from, or abused each other.

Now that we're sober, we have to deal with an area that we were probably never competent at in the first place. We need to develop new attitudes and skills to help repair damaged relationships. We'll encounter several different issues and we should know how best to approach them.

A Family Disease

Addiction is a *family disease*. Our addiction, like a tornado going through a trailer park, has had profound effects on our families and friends. Many of the tougher problems in early sobriety involve the family.

When we were using, our denial let us ignore how we behaved toward those around us. We may still tell ourselves that we were careful not to harm others or that we never let them see us high. This is our addiction and self-centeredness talking. Those who care about us have spent sleepless nights and anxious days wondering if we were all right. When they didn't hear from us, they thought we were dead or in jail.

When we were present, they found that we upset family and friends with our demands and abusive manner. They walked on eggshells hoping not to set off another drinking or drugging episode. They went out of their way to help us—only to find that we had taken advantage of their caring. We stole money, goods, and time from their lives. We created emotional chaos. We never looked back or said we were sorry then. Our focus was exclusively on our chemical use.

As addicts, we tend to dismiss or soft-pedal these consequences of our use. The truth is that we feel ashamed of our past behavior and want to pass quickly over it. We can't ignore this aspect of our recovery. *We must take responsibility for our actions—past and present.* We must be rigorously honest.

☞ *[see example 46]*

When the Relationship Becomes the Focus

Some of us want to rush back to our relationships and move on with our lives. We tell ourselves that if we can make a success of our marriage then we won't have to use chemicals. Our focus is on the relationship not on recovery.

Example 46. Al said that he had not hurt his wife and children since he had never used in front of them. His wife, however, told a different story. She had been home taking care of their four children for many years. When Al's drugging became severe, she was overcome with worry. He had already gone through a large part of their savings. She feared that Al would leave or would die from his chemical use. She saw herself as a single mother of four children with no real job skills, out on the streets, barely getting by on government assistance. This was a frightening thought and certainly not how she had envisioned her life.

What we see as noble efforts are really just a way to make *our* lives more comfortable and to diminish *our* consequences. This is a way of denying the past. It's not that simple. Saying we're sorry isn't enough. We will need to have patience and to do a lot of work to regain the love, caring, and trust we desire. The best way to do that is to work on *our* recovery and to let the family heal.

Some of us will need to consider marital or couples counseling. Normally in recovery, it's preferable to work on ourselves and to gain a knowledge of who we are before engaging in counseling with our partners. Sometimes, however, a high level of tension around the household necessitates taking action sooner.

If we decide to get marital or couples counseling, the therapist we see should be experienced in chemical dependency issues. It may be necessary to include our children in the counseling process. None of our family members has escaped the influence of our addiction.

When Others Don't Seem to Care

Some of us will encounter family members and friends who care nothing about our recovery. They're angry about our past behavior and willing to let us know about it. Sometimes it's better not to try to explain how grand our attempt at recovery is. We accept the anger as one of our consequences and understand that it's not our place to change other people's opinions.

Others won't always understand our addiction. We can't assume that everyone will. To us, our recovery is a miracle. To other people, abstaining from chemical use is the norm. We accept that not everyone will view our recovery as a miracle. Their lack of understanding makes no difference and can't deter us from our path.

When Hopes for Harmony Are Shattered

Some families fantasize that once we stop drinking, the relationship will be wonderful and harmonious. This rarely happens. The first few years of sobriety can be hard on relationships.

We and our partners learned how to deal with one another as the addiction progressed. Although these were not healthy interactions, they established patterns of communicating nevertheless. Now that we've stopped using, these rules no longer apply. This can leave everyone walking on eggshells. None of us knows what works anymore. We need to build a new foundation and to see each other in a new light.

Being Honest

Honesty means not minimizing the anger and disappointment of family and friends. It's about taking responsibility for our behavior and about not blaming others. When we blame others, we avoid taking responsibility for our actions and escape the discomfort of having to change ourselves.

Honesty also means clearing the slate—admitting our wrongs. When we reveal the truth, we shed guilt and shame. We immediately feel better about ourselves.

The question frequently arises, how honest do we need to be? If we need to clean house of our misdeeds, should we confess all our mistakes to our families? While we need to be honest, we also need to be compassionate. Do others really need to hear about every detail of our using? Will we cause more hurt and pain by revealing all?

This is not to say we should ignore or play down past events. If we feel a need to reveal past indiscretions, we can talk to a clergy person or a trusted recovery person. We can forgive ourselves without hurting others. Considering the real purpose of our revelation and processing it with others in recovery will be beneficial.

Earning Trust

We're looking for understanding and forgiveness. Those around us, however, are apprehensive about our "new life." They are intimately aware of our old one and not always quick to forgive and forget. They don't trust us and with good reason. We've disappointed them many times. Sometimes we take offense at their lack of trust. We think now that we're sober, things should be different.

We can't expect our families and friends to trust us immediately. We have to earn trust back. We'll see fear and anxiety in their eyes as they wait for the "other shoe to drop." We find people getting close to smell our breath. They still don't trust us with money. Our families may call to find out if we actually went where we said we were going.

We resent that people check up on us but need to accept that this lack of trust is a consequence of our chemical use. We've earned it. This behavior will continue until our actions convince them differently. Earning the trust of others again may take years.

☞ [see example 47]

Example 47. Juan's pattern of drinking was to call his wife on Friday evening and tell her that the boss had given him extra work and that he would be working late. He would finally come home at 3:00 A.M. hopelessly intoxicated. At his wife's urging, Juan entered a treatment program and stopped his chemical use. After three months, Juan was doing so well that the boss gave him a special project. That Friday, Juan called his wife and told her that the boss had given him extra work and that he would be home late. His wife went through the roof. Juan was angry and offended that she did not believe him. A close friend in recovery said, "I don't blame her. Based on your history, I wouldn't believe you either."

Juan thought that because he was sober others should quit worrying. For his family, it looked like a return to old behavior. They had heard all the promises before. Juan will have to prove over an extended period of time that he deserves trust. Once betrayed, trust is not easily given again.

Some of us carry an incredible amount of shame from hurting so many people with our drug use. How can we ever make it up? It takes time to make complete amends to our families and friends. For now, our biggest gift to them is to stay sober today and to start working a recovery program of personal growth. We can't change the past. We can only change today. It's a matter of *doing the next right thing.* Others will judge us by our actions, not our words.

When Reconciliation Seems Impossible

When we first get sober, some of us may see little hope of reconciliation. We shouldn't make rash decisions about a relationship unless it's an immediate danger to recovery. A relationship needs to go through a rebuilding process. We need to learn communication skills that we don't currently possess and to take responsibility for our past actions. We need to give ourselves and our families time to heal. Talking to a counselor and recovering friends can put our situation in better perspective. We need to be patient and try to make all possible efforts to save the marriage or relationship. Counseling or living apart for a while may help the relationship. Too often, we condemn ourselves later by thinking if only we would have done this or that, we'd still be together. *We need to be sure that, if the relationship is over, we did all we could.* If possible, serious decisions such as divorce should be put on hold.

When Our Spouse or Partner Wants to Leave

Sometimes it's too late; too much hurt has occurred. Our partners may wish us well, but they decide that they can no longer participate in our lives, even in our recovery. While we were stuck in our addiction, they were moving on. It's difficult but essential that we respect their decision. Futile attempts to convince the other person to return create frustration and resentments that can lead us back to chemical use.

When We Want to Leave Our Spouse or Partner

We may have formed some of our relationships on the basis of mutual chemical use. The other person may have no desire to stop his or her abusive or addictive use of chemicals. It becomes obvious that these relationships cannot be maintained if we wish to stay sober.

Many of these relationships are difficult to give up—we may have associated with the people for years. Our tendency will be to try to stay in a "familiar" relationship and to just not use. We tell ourselves that addiction is our problem, not theirs. Or, we may try to convince the other person to stop using and to get help, an approach that is seldom successful.

We're especially vulnerable in these using relationships. We're combining emotional attachment and chemical use. This is a powerful combination for us. Not all relationships can or should be saved.

Handling Divorce

If divorce is inevitable, we try to make the transition as easily and quickly as possible. The healthier our relationship with our past partners, the less the divorce process will strain us and other family members, especially children. We should remember the following points.

- Take responsibility for our part of the problem. It's part of the responsible behavior we need to practice in recovery.
- Make every effort to be involved in the children's lives. They need both parents.
- Get good legal representation or seek the services of a mediator. We need to protect our rights. We're not looking for vengeance or martyrdom.

We may feel a need to give the other person everything we own to "make up" for past behavior. A few months down the line, we're angry and resentful—we blame our ex-spouse because we don't have anything anymore.

At other times, there is so much bitterness that the divorce becomes the means to retaliate—a payback for perceived injustice. No one is willing to give an inch. This leaves both parties angry.

We cannot afford to be saddled with long-standing resentments. Resentments are dangerous for us.

[see example 48]

We need to avoid this scene if at all possible. We can't endure long-term resentment and stay sober. We try for an equitable settlement and move on. Holding out for moral victories over inconsequential matters or trying to punish the other person is not helpful to our recovery. We must detach and move on.

EXERCISE 13a

Do you have a spouse, partner, or significant other? Write down how the relationship could jeopardize your recovery. Then write down how you could handle this situation. Discuss the situation with someone else in recovery. Ask for feedback to get another perspective.

Parenting

Few things can make us feel worse than realizing how much we neglected our children while we were using. We may have believed that our use was isolated enough so as to not affect our children. We find that our children were very aware of changes in our attitude and temperament as our using progressed.

Example 48. *In a discussion about divorce, one member of a recovery group was especially angry about the "injustice" he'd suffered. He banged his fist on the table and ranted about how he'd been taken by his ex-wife. When asked when the divorce had taken place, he answered, "Twenty years ago and I'm still not talking to her."*

Each child is affected differently. Some feel as though they've been "tiptoeing around," hoping not to set off another drunken rage. They feel angry, fearful, and confused. They may have learned to withdraw from us to avoid verbal or physical abuse.

Some children feel they're responsible for family arguments or believe something is wrong with them. Our erratic behavior may have become the model for their own behavior. Some may have suffered a severe reaction to our behavior when we were using. They may need professional counseling to come to grips with the traumatic experiences.

Our initial reaction will be to try to quickly make up for our past behavior. *We need to go slowly.* Pushing too hard for forgiveness will only drive them farther away. We need to show them by example. They've heard too many unfulfilled promises. Becoming involved in their activities and schoolwork and admitting to our mistakes are ways to show we've changed.

If our children are old enough to understand, we can explain our experiences with drugs and alcohol—but we don't need to be too graphic. We might introduce them to Alatot or Alateen, self-help groups for children of people with chemical dependency. In these groups, young people with similar experiences can learn about addiction and how to develop healthy attitudes and relationships.

We can't expect immediate acceptance. Our children may still be living in anger or fear of who we were when we were using chemicals. They learn trust through watching us model a healthy attitude. This takes time.

We need to establish a safe, caring home—one that encourages honesty and talking about feelings. As parents, we can model appropriate ways to express feelings. We counteract our past explosiveness by being consistent in our present behavior and promises.

We also need to talk to our children about their own alcohol and drug use. Children of alcoholics and addicts have a higher risk of developing alcohol and drug addiction. They need to know about this susceptibility. Children have wide exposure to alcohol and other drugs from numerous sources. It's impossible to totally protect them. We can educate them about chemical use. We'll watch for signs of alcohol or drug abuse and take early action before the abuse worsens.

Giving our children the principles of recovery is a wonderful gift. Modeling honesty, patience, acceptance, good judgment and respect for others and properly handling emotions can be a great help in all aspects of their lives.

New Relationships

In early recovery, there is a tendency to rush into new relationships. We feel unsettled by our developing emotions. A new relationship can become a quick and easy way to feel good and to avoid looking at our problems.

Turning to someone else to make us feel good about ourselves is one of the blocks to recovery mentioned in chapter 4. A new relationship enables us to focus on something much more comforting than our problems. Because of this, it's important to avoid new romantic relationships for a year. This gives us time to learn sobriety skills and to think about what we want and need in a healthy relationship.

We hear addicts and alcoholics say, "In early recovery, we don't have relationships, we take hostages." Our own insecurity, neediness, and control issues force us to try to *possess* others. Our dependency switches from a chemical to a person. One can be as dangerous as the other. If the relationship ends or if we feel slighted by the other person, we need another way to feel good. If we haven't taken the time to learn to be responsible for our own happiness by feeling good about ourselves from within, we look for the quickest way to feel better—our chemicals.

We don't have the skills and perspective necessary to have a healthy relationship right now. We're missing the ability to be intimate and to accept another person's right to be an individual. Our relationship with alcohol and other drugs has made us selfish and controlling. It's hard for us to understand this. We believe that our relationship issues are the other person's fault.

Now is the time to focus on ourselves and personal growth. As author and lecturer Earnie Larsen states, "It's not finding the right person, but being the right person." Relationships will come when we're healthy enough to have them.

In spite of numerous warnings, some of us will try to establish new relationships. If so, we need to ask ourselves these questions:

- How strong is my need to be with someone? Is this an obsession in itself?

- Do I have a history of rarely being without a relationship?

- Is there a pattern in the type of people I choose to be with: Do I choose people who abuse or neglect me or that I can control?

If we choose to disregard the advice of others and put our sobriety at risk, we must ask ourselves why we're being so self-destructive. Are we rebelling against being told what to do. Has our arrogance and ego gotten in our way, telling us that we're special? As recovering people, it's important to be honest about our intentions.

We can look at ourselves to see if our relationship is affecting our recovery. Are we spending more time with our new partners than with our recovering friends? Are we attending fewer recovery meetings and other sober activities? Are we venturing into high-risk situations to please that person or making changes in our lifestyle to satisfy relationship needs rather than recovery needs?

List five instances when you put a new relationship ahead of your recovery.

1. _____

2. _____

3. _____

4. _____

5. _____

Sex in Recovery

Renewing or starting sexual contact in early recovery can be an area of great concern. Some of us have used chemicals such as cocaine to enhance our sexual experiences. Heavy alcohol and other drug use may have diminished our sexual response. We used chemicals to overcome our moral values or our sexual inhibitions. In recovery, we're faced with issues and feelings that had been shut off by our state of intoxication.

☞ *[see example 49]*

Example 49. Sally was anxiously awaiting the arrival of her date. This would be her first dating experience in sobriety. Although she had dated extensively, this was the first time she hadn't been drunk before a date. When intoxicated, she found it easy to interact with others. She could be sexually active and not have regrets. Now she doubted that she would feel comfortable being sexual. Her moral values, which had diminished with her chemical use, had now resurfaced. She told herself that she could not handle dating without a drink or two to calm her nerves.

Sally remembered that her therapist had cautioned her about emotional and sexual relationships in early sobriety. She was a beginner at dating when sober. Sally had not yet learned basic intimacy skills.

Our emotional development stops when we start our chemical use. From that point on, we used chemicals to deal with life's difficulties. For some of us, that period was in our early teenage years. We may never have learned the value of friendship or the skills for intimate sharing. We lack the tools needed to be in a healthy relationship.

New Sexual Relationships

As our bodies start to heal, our sexual drive returns or increases. If we're not currently in a sexual relationship, it's wise to focus this energy on recovery. As discussed earlier, compulsive behaviors, such as engaging in relationships during early recovery, can initiate the relapse process. As difficult as it may be, we're better off not getting involved in a new relationship during the first year of recovery.

In the past, sex was our passage to what we believed was intimacy. To feel more comfortable, we chose people who were equally inept at relationships. We thought we could have sex without emotional involvement. If we continue this pattern, our self-worth will get tied up in these relationships. We won't be able to let go and our sobriety will suffer.

We're not really sure how to be friends with other people. In the past, being friends was sharing our drugs or buying the other person a drink. It had nothing to do with honesty and developing social bonds through intimate sharing.

We need to learn to be a friend before we are a lover. Jumping into sexual relationships in early sobriety usually proves unsuccessful. We just don't have the skills or emotional balance for it. Our pursuit of romance and sexual intimacy vastly improves our chances of returning to chemical use. We need to become healthy ourselves so that we have something to "bring to the table" in a relationship.

LET'S SEE: I started drinking and drugging when I was 15, I got sober 2 years ago and now I'm 41. Sooo... that means I'm about 17 emotionally.

Current Sexual Relationships

If we're presently in a relationship, we need to proceed cautiously. Many of us have used chemicals in conjunction with sex for so long that sober sex is a whole new experience. We find ourselves apprehensive without chemicals. The additional stress can make our efforts even more difficult. These fears or the inability to have sex sober has led many of us back to using. These are very intimate areas of our lives and we can be harsh critics of ourselves. We need to talk about these issues even if it feels embarrassing.

Sometimes sex has become a forgotten part of our relationship or was a problem before our chemical use started. Our spouses or partners may have experienced unwanted advances or abusive behavior in our quest for sex while we were using. We need to work on improving the relationship first and keep expectations reasonable. Our partners may not be interested in returning to sexual contact until more trust has built up.

Some of us may have the attitude that we're "entitled" to sex with our partners and push to renew sexual activities. Sex is intimacy between *two* people. We need to respect the desires of the other person. Recovery is about respect of self and others.

If we've been unfaithful, our partners may have bitter resentments about our poorly disguised affairs. They are reluctant to forgive us. They feel betrayed and angry. We shouldn't push the issue. It will take time to ease the apprehension and to work through the anger. It's unrealistic to expect forgiveness just because we're sober. For some, counseling is necessary to resolve sexual issues.

Safe Sex

In spite of warnings to the contrary, some of us will still pursue new sexual relationships in early sobriety. If this is our choice, we must be sure that we're prudent. Sex can be a powerful driving force and one where we make impulsive and possibly hazardous decisions.

We need to place safety first by using condoms and other preventive measures to avoid pregnancy and/or sexually transmitted diseases (STDs). Some people we meet in early sobriety are high-risk for STDs. They may have experienced "blackouts," where they have no memory of what they did. Others may have done intravenous drugs but are reluctant to admit it.

Let's think about it. We've put the terminal disease of addiction into remission. Do we want to find out that we've become HIV-positive through careless behavior in sobriety? We must always err on the side of caution. We may not get a second chance.

Sexually Transmitted Diseases

Our partners may be concerned about sexually transmitted diseases because of real or perceived infidelity or other high-risk behavior on our part. We cannot be sure of the sexual history of our past partners. Our spouse or current partner has a legitimate concern. Saying "It's no big deal, I've been careful" will not resolve the situation.

If we've engaged in high-risk behaviors, it's important to undergo testing for STDs, regardless of whether we have a current partner. We owe it to ourselves and any future partners to make sure of our health. We can't just assume that we're okay.

Pregnancy

Another sexual concern in early sobriety is pregnancy. We don't need the stress of an unplanned pregnancy or an abortion when trying to get sober. There is enough pressure in recovery already. Abstaining from sex is the best choice. Otherwise, we need to discuss birth control *before* engaging in sex, not afterward. Impulsive decisions can yield lifelong consequences.

Inherent Physical Problems

Some of us have done neurological damage to ourselves through our chemical use. When we get sober, we find that we cannot function sexually in a normal manner. Many of us are on medications for depression or other ailments. The side effects can be loss of sexual desire or inability to perform sexually. Some symptoms may decrease in time, but we need to consult our physicians to see if there are solutions to these problems.

Exploring High-Risk Situations

We need to go slow and focus on recovery, not on impulsive sexual desires. When *we* decide *we're* going to do what *we* want to do—regardless of how it affects ourselves or others—it's not long before we're doing what *we* want to do most—use alcohol and other drugs. The exercise of self-will plays a significant role in relapse. We need to identify high-risk situations that could prove dangerous for us.

EXERCISE 13c

List three ways that your sexual craving could place you in danger of a relapse to chemical use.

1. _____

2. _____

3. _____

Remember:

- Waiting about a year to form new romantic relationships will help our sobriety. We should not mistake lust for love.
- If we're in a marriage or committed relationship, we need to be patient and wait to make serious changes.
- Forgiveness and trust have to be earned over time.
- Our families and children have been affected by our addiction.
- We need to detach and move on from relationships that are over.
- Our past behavior and infidelity can have a profound effect on our existing relationships.
- It is important to respect the needs of our partners and not push for sexual intimacy right away.
- We should get tested for sexually transmitted diseases and not assume we're okay.
- Seeking counseling or meeting with our physicians can help to resolve any sexual problems.

Chapter 14

Self-Defeating Beliefs And Behaviors

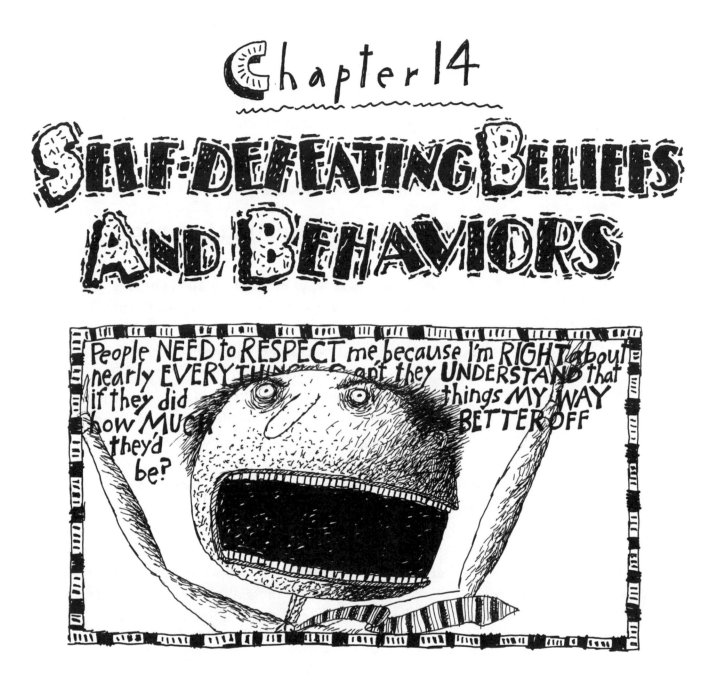

People NEED to RESPECT me because I'm RIGHT about nearly EVERYTHING... cant they UNDERSTAND that if they did things MY WAY how MUCH BETTER OFF they'd be?

 e've made a choice for recovery. We find life is getting better with our abstinence from chemicals. We haven't experienced urges to use alcohol or other drugs. We don't see why we would want to go back to chemical use.

In spite of this positive outlook, some of us do return to chemical use. We acknowledge that life is better without alcohol and other drugs, but we find ourselves slipping back into our old ways.

PERSONAL STORIES

Example 50. *Arlene is checking out at the supermarket. The man in front of her has twelve items but is in the ten-item-or-less line. Now that his total is rung up, he takes out his checkbook and slowly begins to write the check. He spends additional time filling in the check register before handing the check to the clerk. Arlene is angry and impatient. Why couldn't he have gone in the proper line? Why couldn't he have started filling out the check sooner? Why are people so stupid? Anyone who has to put up with these idiots has a right to use chemicals.*

☞▌ *[see example 50]*

Arlene's discomfort comes from self-defeating beliefs. To her, this incident is just another thing going wrong in her life today. She's starting to feel as though the world is out to inconvenience her. The same type of thinking led to her chemical use in the past. Arlene is reverting to her old thinking. She's starting to take the same track again.

The Role of Self-Defeating Behaviors

Stopping chemical use doesn't change negative attitudes and unhealthy behavior. These ways of thinking and behaving have over time become subconscious habits. They are learned traits and defense mechanisms we've used to deal with uncomfortable people and situations. These negative traits help us to avoid responsibility or to escape unpleasant emotional feelings.

As addicts and alcoholics, we are known for doing the same thing over and over, expecting different results. We call this *addictive insanity.* Continuing to use or returning to past self-defeating thinking and behavior is a perfect example of addictive insanity. This mind-set can derail our recovery. We find ourselves justifying a return to chemical use.

Discomfort with personal responsibility or dealing with unpleasant emotions is not new to us. It's one of the reasons we turned to alcohol and other drugs. In recovery, we may find ourselves automatically reacting or behaving negatively to familiar situations, such as being behind a slow driver or having to wait in line when everyone should know we're in a hurry.

We may be unaware of how our behavior influences us. These automatic reactions are powerful, and we're apt to see them as simply part of us. We may believe that they are unchangeable, but changing these beliefs is possible. Not only is it doable, it's a vital part of recovery.

In chapter 8 we saw that our belief system is responsible for our feelings and behavior. If our beliefs are in error, the serenity we seek evades us. We need to change our actions and our thinking. This can be a long process. We will need to practice healthy actions and responses frequently before our deep-seated beliefs start to change.

Common Self-Defeating Beliefs

Here is a list of the more common self-defeating beliefs.

1. I should never be uncomfortable—physically or emotionally.

   Life should be painfree. I must never feel angry, anxious, or depressed. Pain is unacceptable and should be suppressed as quickly as possible.

This kind of thinking is common for us. Quick relief from pain used to come in the form of alcohol and other drugs. We need to accept that life is full of uncomfortable situations. If we don't, we're constantly angry and blaming others for our problems. We feel we're being treated poorly or unfairly. This prompts us to use chemicals to change how we feel.

2. I must never be inconvenienced.

   I can't tolerate being inconvenienced by other people. No one should ever make a mistake. Everyone should take my feelings into consideration. I must have things my own way!

As stated in chapter 9, this is referred to as the king-baby complex: "I want what I want when I want it, and I want it now." Our egos get in the way. We start to believe that we're special. We deny the reality that life is frequently inconvenient. We're filled with anger and become impatient and resentful when others don't do things the way we believe they should. We're unforgiving of mistakes. We've lost our serenity.

3. Life should be fair!

   Fair is defined as things happening "my way." If I win the lottery, that's fair. If you win the lottery, that's not fair. Good things should always happen to me.

Unrealistic expectations of life set us up for disappointment. Life becomes about getting what we want. We become jealous of what others have. But let's think about it. *If life were fair,* we would have been caught every time we drove intoxicated, every time we bought illegal drugs, and every time we lied to someone. Life is unpredictable. It doesn't always play by our rules.

4. I know best. I should be in control.

Other people make me angry and frustrate me when they do things I know are wrong. People should see things my way. If they do not, then I need to change them. You should behave in a manner that is comfortable for me. Sometimes my fear may require me to try to control everything around me just to feel safe.

We need to admit that we don't know everything. When we try to exert control over others, we set ourselves up for failure and feelings of anger. Part of recovery is concluding that we can control what *we* do, not what others do. If we're arrogant enough to believe we should control others, we're arrogant enough to believe we can control our chemical use.

5. I should never have to ask for help.

I should be able to handle situations by myself. Asking for help may mean that I am weak or inadequate. I should never look bad to others. I should be competent, even perfect, in everything I do. If I am not good at something immediately, I feel inadequate. If I can avoid taking risks, I can avoid looking at my perceived inadequacies and feel safe.

Our fear of looking stupid or failing keeps us stuck. If we believe we should never ask for help, we're invariably disappointed in ourselves when we can't solve our problems. We feel overburdened. We lose confidence in our ability, and our self-esteem decreases. In time, we become resentful that others aren't helping us. They *should* know how we feel and what we need. Our anger level increases. *If we're feeling inadequate, we're probably just inexperienced.* We can learn.

6. Rules are for others.

It depends on whether I can get away with it. I should not be inconvenienced. No one should tell me what to do. I should be able to run my life the way I want to.

If we resist following the rules, one of the rules we inevitably end up breaking is the need to stay sober. Our rebelliousness places us in trouble with others. We're out for our own good regardless of the effect on others. Our life lacks the harmony and peace we seek.

Why won't this WORK?!
I'd ask for help, but then people would think I'm just plain STUPID!

7. Other people, places, and things govern how I feel.

   Others are responsible for making my life miserable. You make me angry and upset. Therefore, you must change—not me.

By blaming others for how we feel, we're relieved of the responsibility to change ourselves. As long as they behave the same way, we can react the same way. We remain stuck and resist change. We give the power to control our lives to others. This encourages self-pity and resentment. We are unable to grow until we take responsibility for our actions and our place in life.

Some of us take responsibility for how others feel: when you are unhappy, I am unhappy; if you have problems, I must fix them; your needs come before mine. I am responsible for how you feel. Our job becomes fixing others. If they're sad, it is our job to make them happy. Because others are responsible for how they feel, our attempts prove futile and we think we've failed. Our efforts to change others will invariably be unsuccessful. It's their job to change.

8. I focus on external things to feel good.

   My self-worth is determined by my job, my clothes, my car, how much money I have (or don't have), the woman or man I'm with, where I live, what I look like, etc. If I don't possess material things, I don't feel good. If I achieve and still don't feel good, I strive for more.

When our efforts and successes still don't bring us happiness, we try to achieve even more. Material things and job titles may be short lived and unpredictable, yet we're willing to base our happiness on these external factors. When this proves unsuccessful, we learn that happiness comes from inside ourselves, not from external sources. We learn that we always have our self. To honor and love our self is a worthwhile investment.

9. Everyone should respect me and approve of me.

   A negative statement from even one person can ruin my day. It means I'm no good. I have a great fear of rejection. I personalize comments that others make. My worth as a person is continually on the line. No one should ever criticize me.

We give a lecture to one hundred people. Ninety-nine people think we did wonderfully, but one hates our presentation. Do we spend the night thinking about what we could have done to turn that one person around?

Sometimes this quest for approval is a sign of our own insecurity. We spend our time trying to please everyone else while our own needs go unattended. It keeps us stuck since we'll never get unanimous approval from everyone. Our fragile egos cannot take rejection and we may respond with anger to any challenge. We forget that respect is earned.

I wonder what the boss meant by that remark last week. I don't think he RESPECTS me, and after all I'VE DONE for him!

10. I can avoid responsibility. I boast about how clever I am for taking the easy way out.

    It's too uncomfortable to deal with many of life's difficulties and responsibilities. It's easier to avoid them and blame someone else for my problems. Self-discipline and self-responsibility are too hard for me so I procrastinate. If I whine and act helpless, I find someone else takes care of my responsibilities.

Our fears or our failure to take responsibility for where we are in life keeps us from moving ahead. It's easier to blame others than it is to look at ourselves. It's easier to "disappear" than it is to be where we're needed. We become a victim. Though we never achieve happiness, we never risk failure. By deciding to be safe, we prevent personal growth and achievement.

◇◇◇

Attached to all of these beliefs is an obsession with other people or situations. *We let others "rent space" in our heads.* Rather than deal with the present, we ruminate about our past mistakes or project about future problems. We spend too much time thinking about people and situations we can't change. The past is out of our control, and the future is unpredictable. We spend the present in frustration and fear.

If we continue the same self-defeating behavior over and over again, we must be receiving some kind of reward or payoff. While the payoffs may not be healthy, they are positive enough to keep us putting forth great energy in the wrong places.

[see example 51]

What are Jim's self-defeating behaviors? What could be some of the payoffs for continuing to blame others for his troubles?

Jim has chosen to blame others for his perceived misfortune. He is engaging in behavior 7—believing others are responsible for how he feels. He also is exhibiting behavior 10—taking the victim stance and avoiding responsibility for his behavior.

What are the payoffs for this type of behavior?

- By blaming others, Jim doesn't have to look at his own behavior. He doesn't have to change his behavior because the fault lies with others. He avoids the discomfort of taking responsibility for his behavior.

- He can find a measure of contentment with self-righteous anger. He can tell himself that he's right and that others are bad for making him miserable.

- Jim can get attention and sympathy as he tells his tale of woe to those around him.

- He can avoid taking any risks involved with making changes and avoid being wrong or a failure.

- He avoids facing reality.

Jim's beliefs and behavior create a safe, stable situation for him in a perverse way. By playing the victim, Jim may find someone to come along and *save* him. This may be a way that Jim solicits relationships. As a victim, he attracts a partner who feels comfortable taking care of and fixing others. We have two unhealthy people in an unhealthy relationship. Each feels as though they have found the perfect person.

PERSONAL STORIES

Example 51. Although Jim has six months of sobriety, he continues to feel miserable. He blames his drinking and drug use on his ex-wife. He blames his lack of money on his divorce, although he has not yet found the "time" to search for work. Friends have offered him work, but he rejects their offers by believing that the job is not up to his standards. He feels that other people are constantly badgering him about his life and making him angry. He can't even drive down the street without some jerk driving him crazy. Jim feels like he's stuck in life with no solution.

EXERCISE 14a

Identify some of your self-defeating behaviors. What are the payoffs? Ask others in recovery to help you identify your behaviors and payoffs.

Pick two self-defeating behaviors you most closely identify with.

1. _____

    a. Give an example of how using this thinking or behavior is self-defeating.

    _____

    _____

    b. What are the payoffs for continuing to use this method of thinking or behavior?

    _____

    _____

    c. How can you start to change this thinking or behavior pattern? Ask others in recovery for help in making a plan.

    I can _____

    _____

    _____

2. _____

    a. Give an example of how using this thinking or behavior is self-defeating.

    _____

    _____

    b. What are the payoffs for continuing to use this method of thinking or behavior?

    _____

    _____

    c. How can you start to change this thinking or behavior pattern? Ask others in recovery for help in making a plan.

    I can _____

    _____

    _____

Once we've identified our self-defeating behaviors, shouldn't we be able to stop them easily? Many of these behaviors are deeply ingrained into who we are. It's difficult to see them ourselves. We're unaware that we're even engaging in them.

We need to tell others about the behaviors we've identified and ask for their help in pointing them out to us. This can be uncomfortable at times.

We must also permit others to point out the self-defeating behaviors we haven't identified but that they see in us. We need to accept their observations as part of a learning process. We need to practice healthy behaviors and thinking.

Remember:

- We must make changes in our behavior and thinking. Stopping our chemical use is not enough.
- Some self-defeating beliefs and behaviors may predate our chemical use. Others may result from trying to protect our chemical use.
- Many of us continue self-defeating behaviors without knowing it.
- When we repeat behaviors that distress us, there may be a payoff of some type for continuing that behavior. Payoffs for our self-defeating behavior keep us stuck.
- We shouldn't be discouraged. Everyone, addicted or not, has self-defeating behaviors.
- Once we've identified self-defeating beliefs and behaviors, we need to plan how to change them. Self-defeating behaviors are difficult to resolve alone. We need to ask others for assistance.

NOTES

Chapter 15
Avoiding a Relapse to Chemical Use

The medical definition of a relapse is a return of the signs and symptoms of a particular disease. In addiction, people equate the term *relapse* with starting to drink and drug again. This is inaccurate. Relapse starts long before that point.

Relapse is a *process* that begins with slight and often unseen changes in our thinking, attitude, and behavior. Over a period of time—weeks to years—our attitudes, beliefs, and emotions change to the point where we are convinced, consciously or unconsciously, that a return to chemical use makes sense.

When we reach this point, it's unlikely that we will think about preventive measures when confronted with a using opportunity. Our attitude has already changed. We find that we have little or no defense against the first drink or hit.

- Relapse starts with a subtle change in attitude and thinking.
- Relapse ends when we start using chemicals again.

Relapse prevention explores the changes in attitudes, emotions, and behaviors that we would exhibit *prior* to returning to chemical use or to becoming emotionally unstable.

Addiction is a chronic disease with a tendency for relapse to chemical use. We are susceptible to relapse whether we have many years of sobriety or only a few weeks.

Susceptibility in Early Recovery

Many of us on the recovery road really believe that we won't drink or drug again, yet a large number of us (40 to 60 percent) will return to alcohol and/or other drug use in the first year.

We are especially susceptible to relapse in early recovery. Our stress levels are high as our bodies and minds go through intense emotional and physical changes. We have not had time to develop reliable coping skills for dealing with the emotional roller coaster of life. We can be easily overwhelmed. Our brains are still clouded by years of intoxication.

On the other hand, it's easy to become complacent. We start to feel good about our abstinence from alcohol and other drugs. We minimize the severity of our addiction and the effort needed to stay in recovery. We gradually forget that addiction is an illness that is hardwired into our brains. We believe in the notion that because we know we can't use, we will be able to make intelligent decisions about our use. We find that it doesn't take much to push us back to using again.

In early recovery, many relapses result from our not taking our addiction seriously. We are not convinced that we are addicted. We understand that we've had negative consequences from our chemical use, but we're not yet willing to admit to being powerless. We hang on to a belief that if we understand our addiction, we can master it. Because we think we have some control, we mistakenly put ourselves at risk.

This POWERLESSNESS stuff doesn't apply to me because I've got everything under CONTROL!

Identifying dangerous situations is crucial. We need to be able to quickly identify high-risk situations when we encounter them (see chapter 6). A high-risk situation is

1. any person, place, feeling, or situation connected with using drugs or alcohol or experiencing emotional trauma

2. any time that we are around alcohol or other drugs

3. any place or situation we associate with high stress

The following list shows thinking and behaviors that are "red flags" in early recovery. We need to take these seriously. They are steps on our way back to alcohol and other drug use and must be dealt with immediately.

- *Slippery people and places.* Slippery people and places can grease our slide back to chemical use. People in recovery say, "If you keep going to the barbershop, sooner or later you'll wind up with a haircut." Going back to our old lifestyle involving using people and using places ultimately leads to our return to drugs and alcohol.

- *Dishonesty.* Dishonesty is the way we lived while we were using. We would have said or done anything to prolong our chemical use. Secrets provide a basis for further dishonesty. Being honest with others and ourselves is a significant part of recovery. Honesty holds us accountable and we willingly take responsibility for our behavior.

- *Control.* We have to accept that we can't control other people, places, and things. Anger and resentments block love and serenity from our lives. To maintain recovery, we must do a thorough housecleaning of our resentments and shortcomings.

- *Relationships.* Very few things can spur emotional upheaval more quickly than romantic relationships. Our relationship with a spouse or significant other can send us to terrific heights or incredible emotional lows. Both extremes can be dangerous in early sobriety.

- *Isolation.* Isolation gives us an opportunity to engage in self-pity or to construct irrational thoughts. We need to break out of isolation.

- *Impatience.* Many of us are anxious to move ahead and get on with our lives. We set our expectations too high. When we can't reach our goals, we believe we have failed. We can remember that our serenity is usually inversely proportional to our expectations of others and ourselves; that is, the higher our expectations of others and ourselves, the less serene we seem to be and vice versa.

- *Emotional distress.* Emotional triggers can be especially dangerous since they can seem overwhelming. When feeling overwhelmed, we seek a quick, reliable solution.

- *HALT—Hungry, Angry, Lonely, Tired.* The concept of moderation is sometimes foreign to us. Our addictive thinking and compulsive behavior make it difficult for us to "take it easy" or "keep it simple." We drive ourselves until we become hungry, angry, lonely, and tired, and our self-care deteriorates.

- *Thinking we know it all.* This kind of attitude plays down the effort needed to stay in recovery. We think that "half measures" are adequate to maintain our sobriety. We display reckless behavior by placing ourselves in situations where our sobriety might be compromised.

- *The unexpected.* Life can serve up unexpected problems that create large amounts of stress for us—accidents, divorce, deaths, financial problems, depression, anxiety attacks, family issues, sickness, job instability. We are seldom prepared for these traumas in early recovery.

Explore behaviors that could change your attitudes and return you to chemical use. What negative attitudes do you see in yourself? Think about your answers to the following questions.

- Are you cocky? Angry? Fearful?
- Do you find it easy to feel inadequate and shameful or would you rather be seen as a "know-it-all"?
- Do you worry about getting approval from other people?
- Are you dishonest with others to avoid consequences or to look better in their eyes?

- Are you likely to let others know when you're in trouble and to ask for help?

- Do you believe that you should never make a mistake?

- Are you easily overwhelmed?

- Do you like to be in control?

- Are you impatient with others?

Do you understand why the above behaviors are dangerous?
List your attitudes and behaviors that could be signs of slipping into a relapse.

_____

_____

_____

_____

_____

_____

_____

EXERCISE 15b

What slippery situations might you encounter? Try to identify as many people or places as possible. Look at your social activities, jobs, friends, and family. Are any of these associated with drug or alcohol use? The more you can identify as dangerous, the safer you'll be.

_____

_____

_____

_____

_____

_____

_____

_____

Now that you've identified specific attitudes, people, and situations that could lead you back to chemical use, what is your plan for coping with each of these triggers?

You can lay out a plan similar to the emergency relapse plan outlined later in this chapter. The plan may be as simple as to not associate with these people or to not attend these events. You may want to review chapter 6 for ideas. Remember that no attitude, person, or event is worth a relapse to chemical use.

Example 52. Chuck had talked his way through several treatment programs but struggled with stopping his chemical use. He always had to get back to his job. He needed to make up for lost income. He was too busy to follow the recommendations of professionals in the recovery field. Whenever he returned to drinking and drugging, he always seemed to avoid consequences. When confronted by friends, Chuck promised that he would stop using. People warned him that he would lose his family and prestigious job if he did not take recovery seriously. Chuck's addictive thinking led him to believe that he could control his use and continue to avoid consequences. The next time Chuck used chemicals, Chuck's wife and his employer had had enough. His wife left him and took the children, and his employer fired him.

Recovery Is Not the First Priority; It's the Only Priority

Some of us try to take shortcuts or don't make our recovery *the* priority. It's easy to become too busy to address recovery. We tell ourselves that the kids need our time—time they didn't have when we were using. There is so much to make up for that we must focus on regaining lost ground. We forget that without our abstinence from drugs and alcohol, we will lose those things that we deem valuable.

☞ *[see example 52]*

As others had predicted, Chuck lost his family and job. His addiction fooled him into thinking, "It will never happen to me." He believed that he had control over his chemical use and would stop if things got "really bad." If we accept the power of our addiction, we can prevent further losses in our lives.

We may have to ask ourselves, "What are my priorities? Am I letting my job, family, or compulsive behavior get in the way of my recovery program?"

The Role of Stress in Relapse

Stress can be a critical factor in setting up a return to chemical use. Stress can take a situation that we could normally handle and turn it into a sobriety-threatening nightmare.

Many of us are unaware of the level of stress in our lives. We frequently ignore stress as something we don't have time to deal with. Left unattended, stress can create an unmanageable situation.

Stress Is Cumulative

We may find it difficult to identify long-standing stressors in our lives. If we live downwind from a sewage plant, after a time, the smell becomes normal. In other words, we've known stress for so long, we don't have anything to compare it to.

Examples of stress-inducing situations include

- any time or situation where there is a change—negative or positive *(stress is an inherent factor in all change)*
- any time we're feeling physically ill or dealing with chronic pain
- any time we're feeling hungry, angry, lonely, or tired (HALT)
- any time we're feeling powerless or out of control
- any time we're feeling shameful or inadequate
- any time we're feeling alone and/or hopeless
- any time we're feeling angry and resentful
- any time we're trying to avoid conflict
- any time we're living in fear
- any time we're feeling pressure from others (directly or indirectly) to perform in some preconceived manner

Many of us tend to stuff feelings into our emotional backpack. When we have stuffed too many unresolved emotions into our backpack, its seams rip open and the emotions explode outward at ourselves and others.

EXERCISE 15d

What are high-stress areas in your life? List situations or people that make you feel stressed. (Examples of stressful situations are attending funerals, going through divorce settlements, meeting with an ex-spouse, or appearing for sentencing in a court case.)

If we must be in a high-stress situation, we need to plan for it. We can't tell ourselves, "I'll be okay" or "I haven't felt like using so I'll be able to handle it." We're setting ourselves up.

A plan to handle a high-stress situation includes the following:

- *Prior to the situation.* We can attend extra support meetings ahead of time; set up a list of people we can call before, during, or after the situation; plan to bring someone supportive with us; plan to bring recovery readings; let everyone know about the event—no secrets.

  People say, "If I get into trouble, I'll call someone." This is an answer given by someone who doesn't yet understand the power of the disease. If we get into trouble away from our support system, we may not call anyone. We need to commit to calling people at *specific times*.

- *During the situation.* What problems might we encounter during the situation? How can we respond to these problems in a healthy way? What are our resources for support? If we are going out of town, we can take recovery reading with us and make sure we know where recovery meetings are held. We can make calls to recovering friends to help stabilize us during emotional encounters.

- *After the situation.* We may not allow ourselves to experience the emotional consequences of a stressful situation until we've gotten through it. Plan to contact recovering friends or stay in a safe place immediately after a stressful situation. Our emotional responses may be stronger than we anticipate.

These procedures are not limited to those who are in early sobriety. Regardless of how much recovery time we have, we are in danger of drinking, drugging, or collapsing emotionally in high-stress situations.

What If I'm Exhibiting Signs of Attitude and Behavior Change?

If someone points out a change in our attitude, it's important for us to listen and get specific information. We need to remember that others may see changes that we don't. We need to talk about this information with a mentor or sponsor in recovery and with experienced recovering friends.

- We need to step back and take time to review where we are. Are we becoming complacent?
- We can ask for help from others in recovery in dealing with dry-drunk behaviors.
- We may need to increase our participation in recovery activities and interactions with other recovering people.
- We may choose to get more education on a particular issue in our lives or to get away and relax for a few days.
- We can look at our recovery plan. Are we trying to do too much? Are our expectations too high?
- It may be time to look at old, unresolved emotional issues. We can seek professional care.

What Do I Do If I Relapse to Chemical Use?

Regardless of our best intentions, some of us may return to chemical use. We may be taken completely by surprise. We need to set aside feelings of failure and take action to stop our chemical use. There are steps we can take to keep ourselves as safe as possible if relapse to chemical use occurs.

- If we've just started our use, we must **STOP!**

- If we've been using for a while, we may need professional help for withdrawal. An unsupervised detoxification can be dangerous. We may experience seizures or hallucinations.

- We may be disoriented or confused because of the toxic effect of the chemicals on the brain. We need to work on stabilizing ourselves and remaining safe. Our chance of continuing our chemical use at this time is high. *Safety from continuing our chemical use is the first priority.*

- We can turn to our support system *immediately*—recovery group or friends, aftercare group, counselor or therapist—and let them know what's going on.

  There is no shame in a relapse to chemical use. A relapse is not a moral issue, a sign of weakness, or a failure. It's important to be honest about what has happened. The people around us will appreciate our honesty and support our need to return to recovery. We can't keep secrets in a program based on rigorous honesty and expect to stay sober.

- We work to get past any feelings of failure, anger, guilt, shame, blaming, or self-pity for relapsing. Thoughts of "I should have known better!" can keep us from the help we need. Talking openly about our feelings with other recovering people will make it easier for us to cope.

If we have a pattern of relapsing, we can't take chances. We need to seek professional help. Several different levels of care are available to the person struggling to stay sober. Our medical insurance may cover treatment. If we don't have insurance, we can check with city, county, or state social service organizations.

We should never try to handle a relapse to chemical use alone. We need to ask for help and get others involved. Failing to do so can lead to continued use and to severe consequences. It's easiest to quit immediately.

When we're feeling better, we can start to analyze what feelings or thoughts preceded our use. We don't focus on what other people did or said but rather on how we reacted. "How did I feel?" "What was I thinking?" *Other people, places, or things cannot make us return to chemical use.*

We may have been doing something wrong or omitting something right. We need to go back and look for breaks from our program of recovery or for situations that may have inspired an attitude change. Many times we will return to chemical use by the same method. The people and scenery may be different, but the "play and the ending" are the same.

Others in recovery will be able to see mistakes that we've made. Now is the time to review how the relapse occurred and be willing to change. We need to look closely with the help of others to discover how we end up returning to chemical use. The saying "Doing the same thing over and over again and expecting different results" applies.

✧✧✧

Some of us encounter severe attitude deterioration but do not return to chemical use. We may find ourselves in an emotional crisis. When confronted with a deteriorating attitude and spiritual foundation, some of us have a mental "meltdown." We become overwhelmed emotionally and feel hopeless or in intense pain. We may become suicidal.

We know that we cannot use chemicals, but the emotional pain becomes overwhelming. We need to let others know if we are depressed or suicidal. Getting good mental health professionals involved can save our lives. We need to practice prevention and plan beforehand.

Remember:

- If we relapse to chemical use, we must stop immediately! We need to let others know what's going on.
- If we start to show signs of an attitude change, we need to act to resolve this immediately. Left unchecked, it could lead to alcohol or drug use.
- The power of addiction should never be taken lightly. It's far stronger than we believe it is.
- We can choose not to put ourselves in risky situations. Knowing what constitutes a high-risk situation helps our recovery.
- Getting sober and staying sober require work and some sacrifice.

- We should never get into a contest with our addiction. Testing ourselves to see if we're "strong enough" to handle a high-risk situation is foolish. The disease always wins.
- We avoid thinking we know best. *It's important to be guided by other people.* We know how to use. We don't know how to recover.
- Recovery is a process. We didn't get to where we are overnight and we can't recover quickly either.
- Staying in recovery, especially in the early days, means making hard choices. We may have to leave a job or relationship that's dangerous to our recovery
- Never go into a high-risk situation without a plan. Neglecting to plan for basic safety results in a return to chemical use.

Personal Emergency Relapse Plan

Some of us may be reluctant to write an emergency relapse plan. It's uncomfortable to sit down and think about the possibility of a return to chemical use. It feels much easier to forget it. Out of sight, out of mind.

If we start using chemicals again, most of us are not going to be rational enough to know what to do. It can be frightening to friends and family if we are using drugs or alcohol and they don't know what to do. While it's easy to say, "If I start to have trouble, I'll call someone," we rarely do so.

If we should return to chemical use, we can have a plan already in place. The plan is a contract between us and our families or friends. We become accountable for our actions. The terms may involve going to detox, going to a treatment center, or moving out of the house. These are sometimes harsh measures, but they are a consequence of our own creation. Perhaps the reality of the contract may get us to think before we take chances with our sobriety.

Give copies of your plan to family and recovering friends so you know you'll receive appropriate care. Give them permission to intervene. They will be your first line of defense in identifying early relapse warning signs. Listen to them. You will need them if you return to chemical use. You cannot achieve recovery by yourself.

My Personal Emergency Relapse Plan

A. The people I can call and ask for help are:

1. _____
   NAME   PHONE NUMBER
2. _____
   NAME   PHONE NUMBER
3. _____
   NAME   PHONE NUMBER

B. The places I can go for help are:

1. _____

2. _____

3. _____

C. Thoughts that will motivate me to stop the relapse are:

1. _____

2. _____

3. _____

D. If I am unable or unwilling to take these measures, I agree that I will:

_____

_____

_____

_____

_____

_____
Signature

Give copies of your plan to family and recovering friends so you know you'll receive appropriate care.

NOTES

Chapter 16

PRESCRIPTION AND NON-PRESCRIPTION DRUGS

e've come to accept that we're dependent on mood-altering drugs. But what can we do when we need a medical procedure or a prescription drug?

Addicts in recovery may be faced with medical situations where narcotic or other addictive medications are suggested or necessary for surgery or to manage severe pain. It's important that we're aware of the types of medications we're taking. Some recovering people choose not to take mood-altering medications under any circumstances. Others follow certain rules for medication use. We need to be aware of potential risks in taking prescription drugs.

Example 53. Gina is new in her attempt at abstaining from alcohol and other drugs. In the past, she took mood-altering medications from her sister's medicine cabinet and from a doctor who she knew would give her prescriptions easily. Now she's going to the dentist for an oral surgery appointment. It would be easy to get a narcotic pain medication if she asked. She wonders what she should do. She hates pain!

If the Doctor Prescribed It, It Must Be Safe . . . ?

We remember from chapter 2 that we're susceptible to all mood-altering drugs. This phenomenon is called *cross-addiction.* It doesn't matter whether we're discussing illegal drugs, alcohol, or prescription drugs. They're all the same to the addict. We're always vulnerable. It's up to us to identify situations where we're at risk.

👉 *[see example 53]*

Gina can put a simple plan in place for her protection.

- She can let the dentist know that she's addicted to mood-altering medications.
- She can tell her friends about her appointment and her concerns.
- She can ask a recovering friend to go with her.

We need to be honest with our physician, dentist, and other health care professionals about our alcoholism or other drug addiction. Health care professionals are accustomed to hearing this information and appreciate being informed. To effectively treat us, they need to know about our addiction. Not being honest with them leaves the door open for us to abuse prescribed medications.

If we've seen our doctors and have not told them about our dependency, we have to ask ourselves—why not? Are we leaving that door open to future abuse?

When we do inform our health care professionals, we need to be aware that some of them are unfamiliar with the needs and concerns of dependent people. We may want to believe that if the doctor prescribed a medication, it must be safe for us. This is not necessarily true. Doctors may inadvertently prescribe addictive medications to dependent people, triggering a return to addictive chemical use.

Ultimately, we are responsible for the medications we're taking. We must ask our doctors about the availability of non-mood-altering medications. If we're unsure about the addictive qualities of a medication, we can call the medical unit of an addiction treatment center or a pharmacist for guidance.

When There Are No Alternatives

In chapter 6, we concluded that any time alcohol or other drugs are around, we're in danger of using. If we accept a prescription for a mood-altering medication because there are no alternatives, we cannot simply assume that we will take that medication in the prescribed manner. The medication may trigger a severe response from the brain's pleasure center. Even medications taken according to directions may trigger euphoric recall or using urges.

We must be aware of potential problems and do what we can to keep ourselves safe. We need to

1. let people in our support system know what we're taking and why;
2. give the medication to someone we trust and ask this person to dispense it to us;
3. dispose of any unused portion when we no longer need a medication. Saving medication for a future medical problem is dangerous and assumes that we can control our chemical use. We must flush it immediately to avoid any temptation.

When Family or Friends Are on Medication

Our family members, roommates, or friends may leave their own prescription medications lying around. These people frequently do not understand how powerless we are over our addiction or do not realize we are addicted to all mood-altering substances. They mistakenly believe that these medications will not tempt us.

We may feel uncomfortable about saying anything that will give them the impression that we're not trustworthy. We must resist the temptation to tell ourselves we can handle these situations by ourselves. We need to let others know that we're susceptible to their medications.

What If We Need Hospitalization?

[see example 54]

Hospitalization can be a potentially dangerous time for the alcoholic or addict. When such a visit is necessary, we need to construct a careful plan to identify the risks involved. Carl didn't have a plan of action. He didn't foresee any problem with his hospitalization. After all, he was an alcoholic and had never used other drugs.

PERSONAL STORIES

Example 54. Carl is a recovering alcoholic. Recently he needed major surgery. During his hospitalization he received narcotic pain medications to keep him comfortable. Soon after leaving the hospital, Carl started to drink again. His friends wondered if the two incidents were connected.

In planning for a hospital stay, we should

1. *make sure the physician knows that we're in recovery from addiction.* This may influence the choice in medications prescribed for us. If we're having surgery, we must let the anesthesiologist know about our alcohol or drug dependency. He or she may want to change the anesthesia based on that knowledge. People who have not made a strong commitment to stay off alcohol and other drugs may remain silent in hopes of getting a "legal" prescription for a mood-altering substance. We can't withhold information about ourselves from professionals who need to know.

2. *be aware that we may receive narcotic or mood-altering chemicals as part of our treatment.* These medications, as in Carl's case, may trigger addictive responses. By the time Carl left the hospital, he was already thinking about furthering this high. It just seemed like the right thing to do. Because he was unprepared, he fell victim to his dependency to alcohol and other drugs. The stress of a hospital visit combined with the discomfort of an illness or injury can influence our decision-making processes. We're particularly vulnerable in these situations. This type of reaction is not uncommon and people leaving the hospital are at a higher risk for a return to chemical use. We need to be cautious and be prepared.

Constructing a Simple Plan

When preparing for an upcoming high-risk situation, we should plan our actions before, during, and after the event.

- *Before.* We should let everyone know about the doctor appointment or hospital visit and the possibility of prescription medications before going. No secrets. We must process everything with our recovery support system. This may mean attending extra support meetings prior to our admission.

- *During.* We should have someone go with us to the appointment. It will be important to tell the doctor and other hospital personnel that we're recovering from alcohol or drug addiction. We should be aware that we may experience euphoric recall or using thoughts.

- *After.* We should have someone pick us up from the hospital. We can ask our doctor or pharmacist about the appropriateness of any prescribed medications. Having a safe place to stay for a few days or someone to monitor us afterward is a good idea. Attending more support meetings after the medical procedure is also a good idea.

EXERCISE 16a

Complete this checklist before being hospitalized.

	YES	NO
1. Have you told *all* your health care professionals about your addiction to alcohol and other drugs?		
2. Have you informed your family, recovering friends, and addiction counselor about any prescription or nonprescription drugs you're taking?		
3. Do you or another person have prescription drugs around the house now?		
4. Do you know if any of the medications you're currently taking are potentially addictive?		

We can't be afraid to discuss our vulnerability to prescription medications. Many of us may say that we're only alcoholic and not susceptible to abusing prescription drugs. Let's not be fooled. Many relapses to alcohol use were triggered by playing down the addictive potential of prescription drugs. We must be smart and be aware.

Antidepressants and Other Long-Term Medications

A large number of people who are chemically dependent take antidepressants or antianxiety drugs. Most antidepressant medications are not mood altering and are not addictive. They simply rebalance the brain's neurotransmitters to a normal level.

Some people in recovery discourage the use of any type of medication, but antidepressants are extremely important in maintaining sobriety and peace of mind. People who stop taking their medications may relapse to chemical use when the symptoms of their depression

Example 55. *Mary had two years of sobriety. Like many alcoholics and addicts, she lived by the credo "I should never be uncomfortable, physically or emotionally. If I am, I must end it with all due haste." She had a history of headaches and began routinely taking aspirin for the discomfort. In an attempt to avoid having headaches altogether, Mary started to take aspirin in the morning as soon as she got up, several at noon to avoid any afternoon complications, more at dinner to make it through the evening, and several more before bedtime to make sure she slept well. After all, aspirin was over-the-counter medicine so how powerful could it be?*

or anxiety reoccur. The presence of depression or anxiety inhibits personal growth and increases the possibility of a return to chemical use.

Some drugs used to treat psychological disorders do have the potential for abuse. We may find ourselves needing to take potentially addictive medications for seizures, for attention deficit disorder (ADD), or for other conditions. We shouldn't hesitate to inquire about the nature of the medications we're taking. There may be nonaddictive alternatives.

If we must take an addictive medication for a medical condition, we must be acutely aware of the potential for abuse. Some of these medications enhance addictive thinking. We can inform others of our situation and ask for help in monitoring our behavior and attitudes.

Over-the-Counter Products

🖝 *[see example 55]*

When Mary developed bleeding ulcers, she was forced to rethink her "preventive strategy."

Because people who are chemically dependent are susceptible to compulsive and ritualistic behavior, some start compulsive or "preventive" use of non-mood-altering drugs. Over-the-counter medications can cause problems for those of us who believe that *if a little is good, more is better.* In addition, the decision to use and ultimately to abuse over-the-counter drugs causes some people to slide back into using their drug of choice. We need to be aware of the potential for abusing readily available medications.

Some familiar preparations contain large quantities of alcohol or other nonregulated mood-altering chemicals. A well-known nighttime cold medicine is 10 percent alcohol (20 proof). Nasal decongestants and inhalants may contain stimulants. Some cough medicines and mouthwashes are among the many preparations that can contain alcohol or other potentially dangerous chemicals.

Here are some points to remember when buying over-the-counter products.

- The use of any over-the-counter medications should be discussed with our recovery support system or counselors.
- People who are chemically dependent seem to be very susceptible to ritualized behavior. Taking over-the-counter medications can become a ritual that is comforting and predictable but sometimes dangerous.
- Most over-the-counter medications are meant for use during a brief period. Continued use may be unwise and mask a more serious medical condition.
- Many medications and mouthwashes have safer alternatives. We should consult the pharmacist if we are unsure of the best selection.
- It is best to do without if possible.

Remember:

- We need to be honest with our physician, dentist, or other health care professionals about our alcoholism or drug addiction.
- Everyone in our recovery support system should know about any upcoming doctor or hospital visits. We should prepare beforehand.
- We should never assume that we will be able to take a mood-altering medication as prescribed. We can give it to someone we trust to dispense to us. It's important to flush any remaining medications immediately.
- Medications should be taken in the prescribed manner. We should never stop taking antidepressants or other medications without contacting the physician first.
- Ultimately, we're responsible for the medications we're taking.

NOTES

_____

_____

_____

_____

_____

_____

_____

_____

_____

_____

_____

_____

_____

_____

_____

_____

Chapter 17
The Importance Of Self-Care

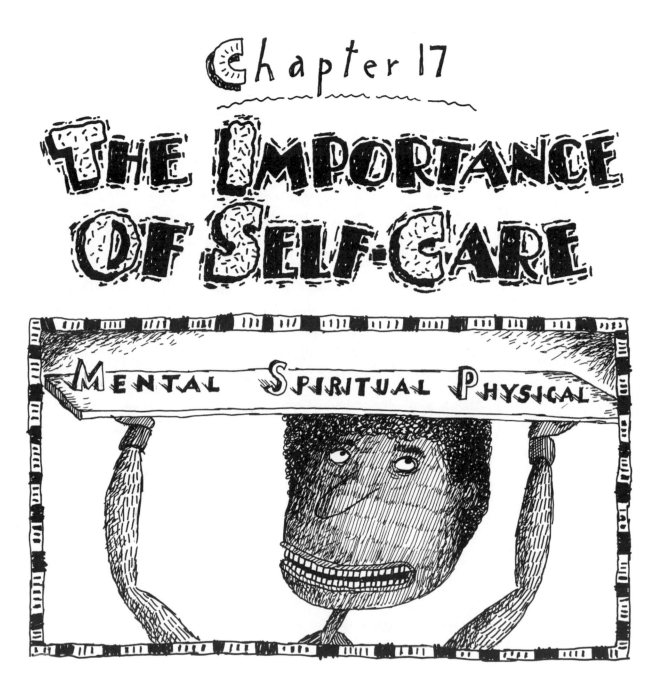

MENTAL   SPIRITUAL   PHYSICAL

 iving a lifestyle of recovery asks us to improve all areas of our lives, not just to stop our chemical use. We're asked to develop moderation—a strange concept for the alcoholic and addict. Usually our living style has been an all-or-none proposition—living on the edge or ignoring everything.

Now we look for balance in our lives. We focus on self-care as part of the solution for keeping us sober. This is a difficult process. We become impatient and want quick results. We need to remember that recovery is a journey, a process that does not happen overnight.

Many of us have neglected our own health needs for years because of our chemical use. Our chemical use may have influenced our eating and sleeping patterns or reduced our physical activity. We postponed or made excuses to avoid health care appointments. We avoided such appointments for fear of hearing bad news. Our focus remained on our alcohol and other drug use, not on our well-being.

Use of alcohol and other drugs can take a heavy toll on psychological and physical health. We need to assess the damage we've done. We need to listen to what others have to say and follow through. We may feel afraid or rebellious. We continue to want to accomplish recovery by ourselves and to not have to ask for help. It's necessary to once again remember our saying, "We need to make our lifestyle fit our recovery, not our recovery fit our lifestyle."

Physical Examinations

It's a good idea to have a comprehensive physical examination after we've gotten sober. In early recovery, we may find ourselves plagued by pains and aches that we never noticed before. Our chemical use may have hidden existing medical conditions or caused new illnesses. A physical examination can identify diabetes, high blood pressure, or other illnesses that may get worse if left untreated.

We can't forget to let the physician know that we're chemically dependent to *all* mood-altering drugs. Sometimes even if we mention that we're alcoholic, a physician may unknowingly prescribe mood-altering prescription drugs. He or she may be unaware of the reality of cross-addiction or of the severity of our dependency. We can't be afraid to ask questions.

Dental Exam

When using, most likely we overlooked dental care. Dental pain may have been another excuse to continue chemical use, or our drug may have masked the pain. When we get sober, these conditions need to be addressed quickly. Severe dental pain can trigger a relapse to chemicals when we decide to use to moderate the discomfort.

We want to consider what type of anesthetic the dentist will be using. Novocaine and other local anesthetics for numbing the teeth and gums should present no addictive problems for the addict and alcoholic. Nitrous oxide, or "laughing gas," is a mood-altering chemical and should be avoided.

Some dentists may administer a tranquilizer to anxious patients prior to treatment. These are usually mood-altering, addictive substances and should be avoided. We can't *assume* that the dentist is making allowances for our chemical dependency in the chemicals he or she prescribes. We must ask!

It is important to make sure the dentist understands addiction. We need to be honest about our chemical dependency. Lack of accountability leaves the door open to obtaining a mood-altering prescription. Once our dental work is complete, we need to be responsible and return for periodic checkups. We need to take responsibility for ourselves. (See also chapter 16 on medication awareness.)

Eye Exam

It's important to get our vision checked periodically. An eye doctor can check for eye problems that we may have ignored during our chemical use.

Visiting a Mental Health Professional

Many alcoholics and addicts have a coexisting mental health condition, such as depression, bipolar disorder, or anxiety disorder. Some of us experience a great deal of stress in our relationships and may need family counseling. We may have started using mood-altering chemicals to mask our emotional issues or to feel less stress.

If someone suggests that we (and our partners and children) see a mental health professional, we need to take the recommendation seriously. It's unlikely that we can stay sober with an untreated mental health problem or by enduring family tension day in and day out.

A *therapist* is a mental health professional—a counselor, psychologist, or social worker—who's trained to help us work through emotional issues in our lives. If we need medications to help us through this time, we'll want to consult a psychiatrist. A *psychiatrist* is a physician who specializes in mental health disorders and can prescribe the necessary medications to help our mental health condition.

Complete the following self-care checklist.

	I need to make an appointment with . . .	My appointment is scheduled for . . .
Physician		
Dentist		
Eye Doctor		
Therapist		
Psychiatrist		

Are there other areas that you need to follow through on? Housing? Specialized counseling? Finding recreational activities? Finding sober social activities? Stress management? Vocational counseling?

Identify, with the help of others, other ways to take care of yourself. Also, note where to find the information or help you need. (For stress, for example, you may want to visit a massage therapist or an acupuncturist. Or, you could do something as simple as exercising, taking a hot bath, or listening to relaxing music.)

1. _____

_____

2. _____

_____

3. _____

_____

4. _____

_____

How Do I Find the Right Health Care Professional?

Some of us may already have a family doctor. If so, we need to consider whether he or she is the right professional for us now that we're sober. Does the doctor understand addiction? The family doctor may have directed us to seek help. It is also possible that the family doctor has been watching our decline for years but has never mentioned alcohol or other drug addiction. Returning to that person may be a poor choice.

Using the following resources, we can find a physician, therapist, or psychiatrist familiar with addiction.

- Ask recovering friends whom they've used and whether they were pleased. Ask them if they thought the person was comfortable and knowledgeable about addiction.

- Call local medical societies and get the names of physicians certified by the American Society of Addiction Medicine. These doctors have received special training in addiction.

- Contact a local treatment center for recommendations.
- Refer to the yellow pages but make sure to mention alcoholism and other drug addiction with whomever we contact.

Once we're sober, we become aware of other issues in our lives that we had avoided. Cross-addictions or compulsive behaviors such as gambling, workaholism, excessive exercise, or an eating disorder can emerge as we struggle to maintain our recovery. We need to identify these problems and make sure they are on the list in exercise 17b.

HALT

Part of self-care is remembering HALT—Hungry, Angry, Lonely, Tired. These four conditions can lead us to relapse.

Hungry

In the past, we probably neglected good nutrition. We went for days without eating while using stimulants, or we subsisted on a sporadic diet of fast foods. Some of us had a chronic case of "the munchies" from smoking pot. Proper nutrition may have been lacking in our lives for years.

In recovery, it's time to take our eating habits into consideration. Regular mealtimes and nutritious meals are essential to our recovery and to regaining our physical and mental health. A physician or a dietitian can help us plan our diet. They can offer sound advice and counseling.

The following are some simple rules to get us started:

- Schedule meals at specific times. Make them a part of a daily routine.
- Cut down on the amount of salt and fats consumed.
- Avoid fast-food restaurants. Most of the food is loaded with fat and salt.
- Avoid snacking between meals.
- Always eat breakfast. Many of us are in the habit having of a quick cup of coffee, a pastry, and a cigarette for breakfast. We need nutrition early in the day to carry us through. We need to make time to have a more substantial, low-fat breakfast with moderate portions.
- Eat more fruits and vegetables.
- Don't overeat.

- Don't make radical changes in weight or figure. Resist fad diets or pumping up with steroids. As people who are chemically dependent, we're impatient and yearn for the quick-and-easy fix.
- Take a daily multiple vitamin. We need to avoid taking large doses of any nutritional supplement and be aware of unregulated health products we're putting in our bodies.
- Be on the alert for an emerging eating disorder. Starving ourselves or bingeing and purging is dangerous. If any symptoms arise, we must seek a health care professional who specializes in eating disorders.

Angry

The radical changes we may be making for successful recovery add stress to our lives. We can become short-tempered and resentful. It's essential that we carry through with any mental health referrals and practice developing a spiritual nature that accepts life on life's terms. (Refer to chapter 9 on dealing with emotions.) Anger can turn into resentment; resentment leads to a relapse to chemical use.

Lonely

When we withdraw and deprive ourselves of human companionship, we miss the connection to others that is so important to our mental and spiritual health. We lose perspective on the world around us. Our minds conjure up irrational and self-defeating thoughts: "My head is a dangerous neighborhood to be in alone." (Refer to chapter 10 on isolation.)

Tired

Stress can be exhausting. The early months in recovery are by definition times of great stress. We're usually spending a lot of energy resolving serious financial, vocational, and relationship issues. We struggle with the discomfort of exploring our own defects of character. We seldom have the skills to cope with the stress all of this can create, giving us further reason to return to chemical use.

Getting a good night's sleep is important. Many times in early recovery our sleep patterns are still influenced by old habits and residual chemical effects. We need to be rested and well fed to make the most of each day. This means getting to bed early. It's not necessary that we watch late-night TV or videos. We're changing to a healthier lifestyle, which includes being alert and rested.

Some of us want to make up for lost time and immediately start long work schedules. Again, we need to resist urges to do too much too fast. We seek to achieve moderation. There is no deadline for our recovery. Life has its own time schedule.

In establishing a stable lifestyle in recovery, we learn to take care of ourselves emotionally and physically. Chapter 11 talked about prayer and meditation. We can practice the meditation techniques discussed there. We need to learn to take time for ourselves—time to put the craziness of the world out of our minds. Courses on meditation or mindfulness—living in the moment—and relaxation or yoga classes are offered in most communities. When we're centered and relaxed, we can accomplish a lot.

Many of us have prided ourselves in never taking a vacation— "There's too much to do." We may squeeze in a few days off every now and then but return early to make sure everything's okay. We must let go of this insanity and self-abuse. It's interesting that most things run fairly well without our constant supervision. We all need time to recuperate from daily stressors. If we refuse, we gradually deteriorate and break down. Emotional or chemical relapse becomes a high probability.

The Need to Exercise

When using, many of us completely neglected our physical condition. We were so preoccupied with using that we may have never made an effort to exercise. We can't underestimate the importance of exercise in maintaining recovery. Some of us may have been used to rigorous exercise but have become complacent. Some of us never got into an exercise routine.

Exercise is a great way to improve how we feel mentally and physically. Mental health professionals see exercise as helpful in combatting depression. Exercise reduces stress and makes us feel better about ourselves and our lives. The fact that we're doing something positive for ourselves can be a boost in itself.

Health clubs provide excellent facilities for those interested in serious physical exercise. Some of us have not yet progressed to that level. Walking can be an excellent form of simple conditioning. Biking, jogging, running, and aerobics all can be effective, if we're willing to do the work.

The big question remains—are we ready to take action? It helps to exercise with a friend and to schedule these activities the same time every day. We can do together what we can't do alone.

EXERCISE 17c

Identify an exercise that you can start immediately. Who could help you accomplish this routine?

_____

_____

_____

_____

How might you try to sabotage your routine?

_____

_____

_____

Recovery Is an Ongoing Process

Emotional growth and abstinence from chemicals are necessary to maintain recovery on a long-term basis. Discipline becomes an important piece of the puzzle.

Some of us have treated self-care like previous attempts at recovery. We start out with great motivation but slip into complacency and stop doing what we need to do. We rationalize that we don't have the time or self-care is just too hard. We may perceive others as worse off than we are. This gives us the opportunity to feel unique and to not follow through.

We need to take advantage of available resources to keep us on track and follow through on recommendations from counselors and therapists. They're experienced in helping us through this new and difficult time in our lives. A sponsor or mentor with years of recovery can guide us through the rough spots. *Millions* of people have been where we are right now. We depend on them for wisdom and knowledge in this difficult period.

Just for today I can depend on others to guide me through my recovery.

Remember:

- We were very hard on our bodies when we were using.
- Self-care is a major part of the recovery process.
- It is essential to follow through with recommendations made by counselors or trusted physicians.
- We need to schedule medical checkups as well as ongoing preventive care.
- Early identification of HALT is essential.
- Exercise is a necessity for our self-care and sustained recovery.

Chapter 18
To the Family

 ddiction is a family disease. One of the hardest aspects of addiction is the chaos the alcoholic or addict brings to the family. Like any other illness, addiction elicits a multitude of emotions from family and friends. We may become rageful at the addict for his or her behavior and the hurt that we've experienced. We fear what the result of the addiction will be. Will that person die from addiction? Will we be left alone? Will we divorce? Will everything work out all right?

We find ourselves confused and unsure of how to handle the problem. If our children are the addicts, no matter what their age, we're particularly concerned. We believe that as parents we should protect our children, but we've been unsuccessful in this case. We wonder what we *should* have done? Is it our fault?

Reading chapter 1, Am I an Addict or Alcoholic? and chapter 2, What Is Chemical Addiction? will help us understand what we're facing, namely, that we can't change the person who is chemically dependent.

When we realize that we can't change the alcoholic or addict, we feel powerless over our own lives. As the disease progresses, the addict puts chemical use before the family. We don't receive the love and caring that we desire in a relationship. We may alternate between fear and rage. Our attitude influences our method of dealing with life itself.

It is essential to recognize that *our* behavior as family members has changed in response to the addicted person's behavior. Following are some examples of what we may have done in response to the addict's behavior.

- We may lie for the addict to either employers or friends. When the addict is trying to shake off the last using binge, we're on the phone to the employer saying, "Bob is sick and can't come to work." We lie to friends when we miss social activities because the addict is too intoxicated to go, or we're afraid that he or she will make a scene. We're caught up in the dishonesty of trying to look good because we're embarrassed that this is happening to us. We end up preserving the secret and allowing the situation to continue unchecked.

- As the addiction worsens, family and friends assume more responsibility around the home or at work. We start to focus on the addict or alcoholic, making sure that he or she stays out of harm's way. We may try to control the alcoholic's behavior and find we are unsuccessful. We end up feeling frustrated and confused. Many of us take this to mean we have not tried hard enough, and we begin another futile attempt to resolve the addiction for the dependent person.

- Some of us will deny that the problem exists. We make excuses to ourselves for the addict's abusive manner. We try to convince ourselves that they're under stress at work or that the situation isn't really all that bad. We hope that if we ignore the problem it will eventually get better. It doesn't.

- As a spouse or partner, it's difficult to have compassion for the addict. Our relationship feels out of control, but we seem unable to change it. We try to explain how angry we are and how serious the situation is only to find ourselves shut out or verbally attacked.

- Frequently the addict or alcoholic blames us for the chaos and his or her chemical use. Many of us come to accept that line of thinking and try harder to be a better person. After all, maybe we do have some responsibility to make things better. We find ourselves unsuccessful and angry for being unable to resolve the problem. Our thinking becomes as crazy as the addict's.

- As we're increasingly frustrated by the insanity of our living situation, we find ourselves withdrawing physically or emotionally. The emotional price of living in the extremely stressed and chaotic lifestyle that has developed is too high.

- A part of us feels that we need to be there for the using person even if the situation is physically, verbally, or emotionally abusive. After all, we've done this for years.

How Do We Stop the Chaos?

Secrecy can be the biggest problem we encounter. We feel unable to let others know about the deteriorating situation in our families. Old family traditions such as not discussing problems with strangers or settling problems within the family come into play. We may believe that having an alcoholic or addict within the family is disgraceful or see it as a personal failure and be unwilling to let others know the truth. We tell ourselves that good families don't have these issues.

When we break this secret of silence, we find that many others have been similarly affected. About one in four families has experienced some type of addiction. We find we are not alone and that we can learn from the experience of others. They have the guidance we need.

When we gain a clearer perspective, we see that we need to "let go," or detach with love. Our efforts to control or fix the alcoholic and addict have proved futile. We stop trying to force the square peg into the round hole.

We learn

- Addiction is an illness, not a choice.
- We didn't cause the addiction, and we can't fix it.
- It's normal to feel angry, embarrassed, and betrayed.
- We can hate the disease of addiction to alcohol and other drugs but love the person who is afflicted with the illness.
- We can support the recovering person in his or her attempt to recover. Support doesn't include continuing to live in fear or abuse. We need to protect ourselves and our children.
- The alcoholic or addict is responsible for his or her own recovery, behavior, and actions. We can't do it for the person.
- Whether the addict successfully recovers or not, we need to work on our own health and happiness. We focus on what we can do to feel better ourselves.
- Our rights are just as important as those of the addicted person.

Sometimes our situation is simply too dangerous to continue living in. We shouldn't hesitate to consider removing the addict who continues to drink or drug in the home. If this isn't possible, we can stay with a friend. Turning to professional counselors and other recovering people for guidance will be of great help.

Women may want to contact a local women's shelter to find out about their rights and get guidance in an abusive situation. We can't trust someone who is still using. We must protect ourselves. Safety comes first. We may find it difficult to talk to someone else about our "dirty laundry." We shouldn't fall into the trap of trying to handle an abusive situation alone. We're simply inexperienced at resolving the serious problems associated with addiction. Others need to help.

If the addict is admitted to a chemical dependency treatment center, we can take advantage of the family program offered at the center. As a friend or family member, we can attend Al-Anon or other self-help support groups. Many social agencies have special groups for members of the addicted family.

Family groups do not focus on the addicted person or on learning to change him or her. These groups concentrate on teaching us to take care of ourselves. We're the benefactors. We learn how much we were "hooked" into the addiction and how emotionally draining and frustrating it became. We discover how to put our anger to better use.

There are resources for us. We can call the community or county mental health service, which can direct us to their own programs or to other helpful organizations. The yellow pages of the phone book contain many resources under alcoholism or drug addiction. For advice on treatment for the addicted person, contact the treatment programs listed. For self-help groups, look in the white pages under Al-Anon or call the organization's national help number for information (1-800-344-2666).

We can't control or fix the person who is chemically dependent, but we do have control over how we choose to react to that person. With guidance, we learn how to detach with love from the addict and alcoholic. We need guidance from others who have been in the same place.

Being Forsaken for Chemicals, Being Forsaken for Recovery

Those of us close to the chemically dependent person know the feeling of always finishing second to chemical use. Alcoholics or addicts are usually not there for us when we need them. We look for nurturing and find rejection. We look for love and find anger. We set what we believe are reasonable expectations and find ourselves disappointed again and again.

The addiction has tremendous power. The addict's need for alcohol and other drugs will always come before family, friends, and finances. It comes before life itself. Dependent people will continue to use in spite of warnings that their use will cause their death. We feel abandoned and helpless.

If our loved one is trying to recover, we may find that he or she is now caught up in recovery. We're still in second place but now to recovery. We're not yet getting the attention and nurturing we deserve.

To the alcoholic or addict, recovery is a life-or-death situation. Deviating from that course may be fatal. We need to have faith in the recovery process and understand that change will not happen as quickly as we would like. *It is easier if we can become involved in the recovery process through reading or family groups.*

Many times in the past the addict has apologized for his or her behavior or gone through periods of little or no chemical use. We can't let ourselves be deceived. The addict or alcoholic may be sober for today, but we've no way of knowing for how long.

We can look for proof of change in the addict's behaviors and attitudes and in his or her acceptance of responsibility on a daily basis. We should look for concrete change, not promises. For instance, if the alcoholic or addict has not been financially responsible before, let's not be too anxious to turn over control of money to him or her. Sobriety does not automatically confer skills that the person did not exhibit in the past. The recovering person needs time to develop skills that we may take for granted.

Should We Have Alcohol or Other Drugs around the House?

A frequent question is the advisability of having mood-altering chemicals around the house. A spouse or partner may say, "This is your problem, not mine. Why should I have to be punished and change how I live?"

It's unwise to have drugs or alcohol around the house when someone is in early recovery. This includes prescription medicine that we're taking. We may have to keep medications in a safe place or carry them with us. Addicts or alcoholics may use even when they don't intend to, and they may use a substance that's not their drug of choice. The attraction of chemicals is that strong. Because addiction is *not* a matter of willpower, the alcoholic and addict are susceptible to temptation.

What We Can Do

- We can be totally honest with ourselves about the severity of use by our spouse, partner, or friend.
- We can seek a self-help group or individual counseling for our problems.
- We can take care of ourselves.
- We can know that we aren't responsible for the alcoholic or addict.
- We can stop enabling the alcoholic or addict by allowing him or her to continue to use without consequences. We decide we'll no longer lie for the person or buffer consequences.
- We may have to take extraordinary measures, such as family intervention, court commitment to a treatment facility, separation, or divorce.

We understand that resolving these issues is frightening to us. Even if the addict is no longer using, we're still confused, caught up in the chaos left behind. We can talk at length to a counselor and knowledgeable friends before taking any decisive actions. It may be especially difficult for us if we've isolated ourselves from those who care about us. This is not a task done alone. We need to gain courage and guidance from others to confront these matters.

What We Can't Do

- We can't continue to deny the effect the addict or alcoholic has had on ourselves and our lifestyles.
- We can't blame ourselves for the addiction. Addiction is an illness of body and spirit. We can't cause it. We can't fix it.
- We can't continue to expose our children to the chaos and abuse that frequently come with a dependent person in the household.
- We can't enable the alcoholic or addict to continue his or her use of chemicals.
- We can't spend our lives focused on the abusive or addicted person.
- We can't continue living with the insanity of addiction.

Just as addicts or alcoholics need to focus on their recovery, we need to focus on ourselves and our own growth.

Remember:

- Addiction is a family disease. Every family member is affected.
- We didn't cause the addiction and we can't fix it. The dependent person needs to take responsibility for his or her recovery.
- Our focus needs to be on ourselves. We've progressed into unhealthy thinking and actions as a result of trying to help our addicted family members.
- Help and guidance are essential. Specialists in family recovery are available. We can turn to self-help groups for ongoing care.
- It's unwise to have mood-altering chemicals around the house.
- *We need to let go.*

> *Just as addicts or alcoholics need to focus on their recovery, we need to focus on ourselves and our own growth.*

NOTES

Chapter 19
A New Way To Live

 et's be honest. When we look back at our drinking and drugging days, there are some good memories. For most of us, those times happened early in our chemical use. As our illness progressed, good times became fewer and fewer. We started to experience negative consequences from our use. Our families and friends were affected. The wonderful state of intoxication that we experienced was lost—not to be regained. Had we continued our chemical use, our lives may have been lost. Many have suffered that fate.

As much as we may miss "the good old days," we've found something better in recovery. What we've found is peace and freedom. We no longer have to try to keep our lies straight. A program of rigorous honesty means that we can live free of anxieties and fears. The nightmares and insecurities that plagued us begin to dissipate. We're no longer apprehensive of a police siren behind us. We've nothing to hide. We let people know how we feel. We're no longer an enigma.

We follow principles of recovery:

- Abstinence from mood-altering chemicals
- Honesty in our dealings with self and others
- Acceptance of the things we cannot change
- Elimination of resentments
- Maintaining humility and a willingness to ask for help or to admit our mistakes
- Developing a spiritual nature in how we relate to the world and others
- Relinquishing control to a Higher Power
- Taking time for prayer or meditation to clear our minds
- Living life on life's terms
- Showing acceptance and kindness to others regardless of the differences we may have
- Willingness to do whatever it takes to stay sober
- Seeing our sobriety as a gift
- Developing an attitude of gratitude for our new lives

Living in Reality

It's irrational to think that "bad" things will never happen to us because we're maintaining our recovery. Life is full of ups and downs. We'll continue to experience the hurt and grief of life—a lost relationship, the death of a close friend or family member, sickness, job loss, and days where nothing seems to go right.

We've now developed the skills to cope with life without resorting to chemical use. When we allow ourselves to feel sorrow, we're also able to know joy. Many of us say we were always on the outside looking in—never feeling a part of anything. Now we're part of a recovery community. We can reach out to others.

Let's think about it. We're chemically free. We remember where we've been and what we've done. Many hours a week are spent on improving the quality of our character in order to stay sober. We read daily meditations or recovery literature to keep us on a path of honesty and integrity. We associate with recovering friends who help us move forward and grow in our lives. We get respect from those around us because we're living life as it was meant to be lived. Our spiritual growth and the support of others carry us through.

We'll find ourselves occasionally taking a step backward, returning to old thinking and behavior. *This is a normal part of the recovery process.* We need to reread those chapters that address the areas where we find ourselves stuck. We know that if our old ways begin to surface, we must take immediate steps to remove them or a return to chemical use can't be far away. A thorough program of recovery and honesty can keep them at bay.

We can have serenity and a new life. The very illness that created so much trouble has the capacity to create just as much abundance. Impatience is replaced by acceptance. Our self-respect returns. We're able to forgive ourselves for past mistakes. We keep our expectations of ourselves and others reasonable. We no longer feel the need to judge other people or circumstances.

The price of recovery is a willingness to work a program of personal growth and abstinence for the rest of our lives. This seems like a tall order. We can take our lives a day at a time. We no longer dwell in the past nor try to predict the future. We simply do the next right thing throughout *this* day. We gain self-esteem by doing *esteemable things*. Our lives have changed. We no longer try to make our recovery fit our lifestyle; we find that our lifestyle has changed to fit our recovery.

This journey is a long and difficult one, but the rewards are great. We can reach out and feel the warmth of the companionship of other recovering people as we walk the path together. It all starts with a simple decision on our part to *stop the chaos* once and for all.

We find that our lifestyle has changed to fit our recovery.

⊠ HAZELDEN®

INFORMATION & EDUCATIONAL SERVICES

Hazelden Information and Educational Services is a division of the Hazelden Foundation, a not-for-profit organization. Since 1949, Hazelden has been a leader in promoting the dignity and treatment of people afflicted with the disease of chemical dependency.

The mission of the foundation is to improve the quality of life for individuals, families, and communities by providing a national continuum of information, education, and recovery services that are widely accessible; to advance the field through research and training; and to improve our quality and effectiveness through continuous improvement and innovation.

Stemming from that, the mission of this division is to provide quality information and support to people wherever they may be in their personal journey—from education and early intervention, through treatment and recovery, to personal and spiritual growth.

Although our treatment programs do not necessarily use everything Hazelden publishes, our bibliotherapeutic materials support our mission and the Twelve Step philosophy upon which it is based. We encourage your comments and feedback.

The headquarters of the Hazelden Foundation are in Center City, Minnesota. Additional treatment facilities are located in Chicago, Illinois; New York, New York; Plymouth, Minnesota; St. Paul, Minnesota; and West Palm Beach, Florida. At these sites, we provide a continuum of care for men and women of all ages. Our Plymouth facility is designed specifically for youth and families.

For more information on Hazelden, please call **1-800-257-7800.** Or you may access our World Wide Web site on the Internet at **www.hazelden.org.**